Thinking Just Hurts the Team

Find Happiness and Ignite Your Full
Potential by Taking the Principles
of Yoga to the Workplace

Salisa R. Roberts

ARCHWAY
PUBLISHING

Archway Publishing books may be ordered through booksellers or by contacting:

Archway Publishing
1663 Liberty Drive
Bloomington, IN 47403
www.archwaypublishing.com
1 (888) 242-5904

ISBN: 978-1-4808-5027-9 (sc)
ISBN: 978-1-4808-5026-2 (hc)
ISBN: 978-1-4808-5028-6 (e)

Library of Congress Control Number: 2017954562

Print information available on the last page.

Archway Publishing rev. date: 09/25/2017

This book is dedicated to my husband, Mark. Thank you for always believing in me and letting me take risks. I appreciate you giving me the space and encouragement I need to be me. I also appreciate your reminding me from the beginning that thinking just hurts the team! It means something different to you than it means to me, but I love you for telling me that.

Contents

Acknowledgments

I have a lot of people to thank who contributed to the idea and creation of this book. The project took a village. I would like to start with my husband, Mark, and my whole family. Starting in the fall of 2015, I dedicated my Sundays to writing. Mark and my entire family were supportive in giving me the time and space needed to work on making my dream come true. A special shout-out to my brother Matt for trusting me to share his experiences with the world.

I also appreciate the love and support my mom has given me. She has been my biggest fan since day one. She also gave me my beautiful name. My strength and fierce determination come from my mom. She always reminds me that I can do anything for a moment.

Thank you to my dear friend Donna Drury and her husband Tom. They both encouraged me and kept me laughing along the way.

I would like to thank Gary Olson and his beautiful wife,

Claudia. They own and operate The Ashram yoga studios in Bellevue and Kirkland, Washington. I have practiced yoga up and down the West Coast of the United States. Gary and The Ashram are very special. I hear Gary's voice in my head coaching me all the time. Gary, you're a special person with a unique gift. Thank you for sharing it with all of us. I appreciate your willingness to help anyone willing to help himself or herself. Gary and his team shared many of the phrases, principles, and words to live by in this book.

Thank you to Beth Mooney. It's true that she is the first woman to run a top 20 bank in the United States. She shows us with her actions, not just her words, what a great leader is. I appreciate her willingness to speak up about the importance of our sliding to the right side of our brains and embracing our authentic selves. I admire her grit, determination, and humor.

Thank you to my amazing, awesome partner at work, Heather Henderson. Heather was there every step of the way to bounce ideas off of and make sure I didn't lose my mind. I can always count on Heather to speak her mind and make everything she touches better than how she found it.

I am so lucky to have known and worked with Shelley Frank. He was so good and gone way too soon. I feel grateful for the huge impact Shelley made on my life both personally and professionally. He always challenged me to keep raising my lid. I am better having met, worked with, and known Shelley.

Mark Crowley, you also show up in the pages of my book. I have learned so much from you. Thank you for your generosity and willingness to share. I miss hearing your laugh on a regular basis.

I remember the first time I saw Don Connelly speak. I was hooked immediately. Don, you're another one of the influential voices I hear in my head. Thank you for what you do.

Peter Avolio, you always made me laugh in class. I loved that you had no rules in your class. I miss you and hope you will teach again soon.

Mary Thomas, thank you for telling me I was born divine. You were the teacher who was there when students needed you. I always look back on my time with you and appreciate that you put me on the right path.

A huge shout-out to all the yoga teachers I have had the privilege to work with along the way. You know who you are. This includes but is not limited to Gary Olson, Claudia Olson, Rayne Nahajski, Davin Aslin, and the entire team at The Ashram Kirkland and Bellevue. Thank you also to Tina Templeman, Krist Geriene, Carolyn Sachs-Okonek, Johanna, Mary Thomas, Carmen Greenleaf and Peter Avolio. A special thank-you to René Quenell for telling me that I was full of *pitta*! You were so right! (According to Ayurveda medicine, three *doshas*, or biological energies, are in the human mind and body; pitta is associated with fire, vata is associated with air, and kapha is associated with water.) I have left out some yoga teachers in name, but you are with me in spirit.

To Marc Vosen and Jay Coon, thank you for hiring me and always encouraging me. Jay Coon and Jeff Range always keep me laughing, and I appreciate you both. Go Cubs!

Norm Levy, thank you for telling me that I would be great if I dared to be myself. That was great advice your mom gave you. Thank you for sharing it with me.

Thank you to Darcy Burns-Jelcz and Shawna Rexroat for letting me share your story. Thank you for not giving up. You both raised your own lid that day by not giving up. You both are stronger than each of you knows.

Lena Hirschler, thank you for being you. Thank you for being the first person to read my whole book and give me feedback. You're a beautiful person inside and out, and I appreciate your feedback and positive encouragement.

Thank you, Marty Kers, for also reading my book and getting your friend to take the first fifty copies! You helped me see things I didn't see on my own.

Jenn and Russ Robinette, thank you for the time and care you took with our pictures. I was touched by the amount of care and effort you took in making sure the images were perfect.

Eva Strickland, thank you for thinking about things and sending reading and articles my way. Thank you to Laurie Ovesen for double-checking me and making sure I did things right and included everyone.

I also want to thank the team at Archway Publishing for helping make sure everything was right. You have been terrific to work with.

Lastly, thank you to the team I get to work with and lead every day. You help me get better and stronger every day. I appreciate each of you more than you know.

Introduction

In July 2015, I attended leadership training in Cleveland, Ohio. The CEO of the company I work for came to work with our group. The message I walked away with was that the future leaders of tomorrow are folks who can get out of the left side of their brain and slide to the right. The left side of the brain is the processor, or the thinking side of the brain. It's critical in business to be able to analyze data, organize information, and problem solve. So much of formal business education and corporate training centers on building and reinforcing left-brain functionality. The left-brain thinking skills are hard skills.

The right side of the brain is responsible for relating to others—the people skills. These skills include sensing or reading people and relating to others. I've always referred to these skills as *soft skills*. I have long known that my soft skills are as developed as if not stronger than my hard skills. I didn't talk a lot about this with others, but I quietly knew this was one of the secrets of my success.

Maya Angelou said it perfectly: "At the end of the day people won't remember what you said or did, they will remember how you made them feel." Angelou meant that it doesn't matter what you know or how developed your hard skills are if you don't successfully connect with people. In my world, connecting with people and helping people take action is where the rubber hits the road.

The other point that my CEO made that day at training was that we need to embrace and celebrate our authentic selves. We need to be proud to be who we are and comfortable bringing our authentic selves to work. I left the training empowered by what I heard. I finally felt things like self-awareness and mindfulness had a rightful place in the professional environment and workplace.

I work a lot and love my job and role as a leader. I have a lot of demands on me at work and a lot of stress that I have to manage. In 2001, I started doing yoga. For those of you new to yoga, I will offer a couple of definitions as a baseline to begin understanding what yoga is. In *Light on Yoga*, B.K.S Iyengar said "Yoga is the method by which the restless mind is calmed and the energy directed into constructive channels (Iyengar 1979, 20). An easy to understand definition comes from Yoga.org.nz, "The word 'yoga' comes from the Sanskrit root yuj, which means, 'to join' or 'to yoke.'" The definition goes on to say, "Yoga is a practical aid, not a religion. Yoga is the ancient art based on a harmonizing system of development for the body, mind, and spirit. The continued practice of yoga will lead you to a sense of peace and well-being." One more definition before we move on: A *yogi* is defined as someone who follows the path of yoga on a regular basis.

I use yoga as a tool to find my balance and to relax. Back in 2013, I attended a yoga teacher training at my yoga studio, The Ashram in Kirkland, Washington. I viewed the teacher training through my filter as a leader at work. I started to casually tease my yoga teacher, Gary Olson, that we could rebrand him as a performance coach.

As I walked away from the leadership training in Cleveland, I once again felt empowered to raise this notion of performance coaching with Gary. He asked me to expand on exactly what I meant by these comments. I thought it best to sit down and write about the lessons I learned in the yoga room and how I could apply those lessons in the boardroom. This is when I realized my two worlds were colliding. I joked to myself that Gary wouldn't want to get a one-hundred-page document from me about what I was proposing. That's when it hit me: this was a great idea for a book. Writing a book was one of my bucket list goals. I knew I would start writing when I had something to say. The time is right, and I have a lot to say.

The book started with a simple thought: that I would take the lessons I learned in the yoga room and apply them in the workplace, specifically in the boardroom. The project emerged as a book about leading yourself and becoming the best version of yourself. Life is hard and can knock you down. Yoga helps me reach into myself and bring out, highlight, and celebrate the very best parts of me. To effectively lead people, you have to start by being the best version of yourself you can be.

Thinking Just Hurts the Team is about my personal journey on my mat and in the corporate environment. I have included my experiences of dealing with depression, getting knocked down, and dealing with uncertainty. Through my experience on my mat, I have learned to relax, let go, and find my balance. This has helped me feel well, balanced, and happy. When I am happy and at peace with my authentic self, I can feel content in my personal life and drive more success in my professional life.

The primary reason I practice yoga is for relaxation because I needed to learn to rest. Practicing yoga also helps regulate all the systems of my body and promotes a general sense of well-being. Prior to having yoga in my life, I'd work so hard I'd wear myself out. The universe would step in and make me sick. The universe would force a time-out so that I'd take some downtime and take care of myself. I'd emerge from the state weak, and the destructive cycle would repeat itself. Now, I'm rarely sick because I practice great self-care. I practice yoga three to five times a week. I work with weights a couple of times a week. I eat well, sleep well, and get the hydration my mind and body need. At the time of this writing, I am forty-six years old and in the best shape of my life, in both mind and body.

I've also learned about the benefits of intentional pauses both in yoga and in the workplace. It's healthy and productive to take intentional pauses and breaks from the action to clear your mind. Intentional pauses and breaks refresh your mind and spirit. They make you a better leader who offers a fresh and perhaps different perspective. It took me a long time to have this realization.

I witnessed the refreshing power of such a pause in November 2016 when the Chicago Cubs defeated the Cleveland Indians to win the World Series. I am not a big baseball fan, but I happened to be in Chicago the week this happened. It fascinated me to observe the seventeen-minute rain delay. I strongly believe that pause allowed the Chicago Cubs to gather themselves, reflect, plan, and change the energy around the end of game seven and come up winners. That is the power of a pause used wisely. A pause used wisely can be a game changer.

I would like to take a different kind of pause here and highlight that I'm not a doctor or medical professional of any kind. What I am is someone who has worked really hard to get in tune with what my mind and body need at any given moment. Yoga has helped me become more self-aware. This has been the right course of action for me. Before you embark on a journey into yoga or any change in your overall fitness plan, it's wise to talk with your medical professional. If you are dealing with thoughts or feelings that make you feel unwell or depressed, make sure you get the care and advice you need from a skilled medical professional.

Thinking Just Hurts the Team is the title of this book. I worked with several different titles, but this one stuck; it felt right. Let me be clear: I love to think. Our ability to think and reason is one of the best experiences of being human. The title *Thinking Just Hurts the Team* underscores that thinking or thinking too much can and does inhibit doing things and taking action. I think about doing a lot of different things. I am sure you do as well. It's an entirely different thing to get off the couch and go make something happen or learn to do something well.

You can't just think about success; you have to be willing to start doing what is necessary to make your dreams and goals come true. You have to be willing to put in the effort necessary to master what you want to be good at. When you overthink things, you disrupt your ability to find your flow. I've heard flow described as being in the zone. When you find flow or you are in the zone, you really connect to yourself and what you are doing; you're fully present. You are in union. For me, I find this in yoga, but you can find this state in whatever you enjoy doing.

When I was a little girl, I could get lost for hours in working on a new dance technique or acrobatic trick. I would run down a gym mat thousands of times with boundless energy and hurl myself into the air. I did that because I found my flow. I was in the zone. I got lost in time and space, just living in the moment. Those are the moments when I feel alive, when we feel alive. To get the most out of those precious moments that life has to offer, we have to stop thinking and just do, and then we'll eventually learn how to just be.

Chapter 1: *This Little Light of Mine, I'm Gonna Let It Shine*

Namaste.

Namaste is said at the conclusion of a yoga class to bring the class to a close. Namaste means different things to different people. My interpretation of Namaste is *The light in me honors the light in you.* Acknowledging the light in yourself and bowing to the light in others is a great place to start this conversation.

Think of the light as a pilot light or a spark. It's more like a flame than a light. A pilot light is an ignition source for something more powerful. I have always known a flame burns inside me, a smoldering fire. I dream big dreams and know I'm capable of more than I'm doing—capable of greatness. And so are you. The first key to accessing your flame is believing in yourself. It's important to protect your flame and learn how to direct your spark the right way. Those are the first steps of your journey. If you listen closely, you'll find many songs that refer to touching your flame. Your flame touches that creative place that exists in every one of us, telling us to go where we've never gone before, even if we feel scared or we don't know what we are really capable of. That certainly was true for me as I started on my journey.

If you've ever tried to start a fire, you know how important it is to protect the flame. If you stay mindful of the flame, let it grow, and protect it, you can learn to direct the flame into a fire. A flame that you don't protect and direct can easily rage out of control. An uncontrolled fire is one of the scariest, most destructive forces on the planet. Also, if you don't protect and direct a flame, it can easily get choked off or snuffed out, perhaps forever. If you let a flame go out before it's directed properly, you have to start the whole ignition process over again.

This process is the same for human beings. The vast majority of us are capable of more than we give ourselves credit for. There is an interesting difference when it comes to human beings, though. If you're willing to do the hard work, you'll get amazing rewards along the journey. You've likely heard this before, but it bears repeating: success isn't just about reaching the destination; it's all about the journey. Amazing rewards happen along your personal journey, not just at the end when you get to your destination. The rewards can include actual rewards, awards, and money. They also include joy, happiness, contentment, and growth as you learn from your journey and apply what you've learned from your missteps or misfires to your future endeavors. I have worked for and earned many, if not most, of the good things in my life.

It's up to each of us to own the choices and decisions we make on our journeys. It's important that you make conscious decisions about your life. All your choices and decisions contribute to where you go in life. If you make conscious decisions, then you shouldn't feel disappointed if you aren't where you want to be in your life. This includes not making enough money, not getting enough respect, and not feeling fulfilled or happy. It's up to you to be the change you want to see. Your life is all about the choices you make.

We need to own our choices and decisions, good and bad. I am a product of all the choices and decisions I have made along my journey. Sadly, many people aren't willing to put in the time and effort it takes to get good at the things they want to be good at. Anything good in life worth doing is hard. There, I've said it, and it's a truth of mine. It's easier to sit on the couch and watch TV or surf the Internet than it is to go out and make your dreams come true. It's easier to sit lost in thought, dreaming about what you want to happen, than to get up and do something about it.

The good news is that you have steps you can take to improve your self-motivation. Charles Duhigg wrote a book called *Smarter Faster Better: The Transformative Power of Real Productivity*. Here is what Duhigg says in his fascinating book: "Motivation is more like a skill, akin to reading or writing, that can be learned and honed. Scientists have found that people can get better at self-motivation if they practice the right way. The trick, researchers say, is realizing that a prerequisite to motivation is believing we have authority over our actions and surroundings" (Duhigg 2016, 297).

The decisions to act boil down to ensuring we feel that we

have control over our own actions. The good news is that with practice, you can improve your self-motivation skills. But the whole process takes discipline and hard work. What do you do when no one is looking?

In the book *Essentialism: The Disciplined Pursuit of Less*, Greg McKeown talks about Michael Phelps and his Olympic pursuits. McKeown says, "As we all know, Phelps won the record eight gold medals at the 2008 Beijing Olympics" (McKeown 2014, 204). Phelps continued to impress the world by coming out of retirement to compete in the 2016 Rio Olympics, winning another five gold medals. His will to win—his grit—was on full display during the final Rio races when it looked as if he had trouble pulling himself out of the pool after winning. He clearly deployed all his energy and focus in winning each race at hand. He put all the juice he had into that endeavor.

Phelps became a champion when no one but his coach was watching. He didn't become a champion by stepping on any of the podiums to have the medals placed over his head. The medals were the reward and validation for all his hard work in the pool and gym over the years. He did all the hard work when no one was looking. What you do when no one is looking makes all the difference when you go after anything in life worth doing.

Chapter 2: *The Importance of Experience*

Good judgment comes from experience, and a lot of that comes from bad judgment.

—*Will Rogers*

A good life is experience based. There's no substitute for experience. You just have to get out there and get it. This is true for anything worth doing, personally or professionally. You can't sit on the couch and learn to swim, play golf, do yoga, or prepare for a job in sales. You have to immerse yourself in the experience to get experience. With that experience, you learn and gain confidence in what you're doing. No one can do this work for you. There isn't a pill you can take or a video game you can play as a substitute to get those experiences.

I get it, though; putting yourself out there is scary. Entering a new situation is uncomfortable. But you must recognize and accept that challenge. This is how you continue to grow, evolve, and stay relevant. You have to be willing to go after what you really want. You leave growth opportunities on the table if you don't go after what you really want in life. Follow the advice in the Nike slogan: "Just do it."

Reading is one of the great joys of my life. I have enjoyed reading books by lots of successful people, including Nick Murray. In *The Game of Numbers*, Murray says, "We can always learn by doing. We can never do by learning" (Murray 2010, 21). Murray means that you do your way to knowing; you don't know your way to doing. You gain experience by having experience. There is no substitute for this truth, and it only works in one direction.

A former colleague of mine, Mark Crowley, introduced me to the insightful term *excusal excellence*. We've all heard people explain away their performance shortcomings by saying things like "We would have exceeded our goals this year if it hadn't been for the company's poor marketing" or "I would have met all your important deadlines had I not been asked to attend so many meetings." The truth is all of us can make great excuses for why we failed to achieve excellent results. But only people who fully commit to a goal and let no obstacles stand in their way achieve true excellence. In other words, if you want to get better at something worth doing, you just have to go do it.

In 2006, my work position was eliminated along with those of about twenty of my peers across the United States. It was a scary time. I knew I would land on my feet, but the uncertainty threw me for a loop. Although roughly twenty positions were eliminated, six new roles were created. I felt fairly certain that I had a lock on one of the six new positions. These six new positions were similar to my current situation. I didn't want one of the six new positions; I wanted to take the next step in my career progression. I am a hard worker, and I have always gone after what I want. At no time in my career have I put my full weight and drive into an endeavor and failed. I felt ready for the next step in my career.

I worked for a Fortune 500 company during that time. I had been with the company for twelve or thirteen years. The part of the company I worked for was headquartered in Irvine, California. Changes were happening, but big changes like that never seem to happen quickly. When our roles were eliminated, a funny thing happened: everyone disappeared. That's not how I'm wired, though. I showed up every day until I was asked not to come back. I kept doing what needed to be done when literally no one was looking. Business still needed to get done. My team still needed my help. This wasn't a conscious strategy; things just needed to get done.

I also started to plan for my transition. I had a plan A and a plan B. My plan A was to get promoted. My plan B was to pivot gracefully into one of the six new positions. Failure was not an option. I knew I would survive this change. The best people always land on their feet. I was vocal about wanting to get promoted. I wanted to take on more and felt ready. I felt I had nothing to lose by being more outspoken and advocating for what I wanted.

Early on in this process, one of the head guys from Irvine

invited me to dinner. We had a great relationship. He used to be my boss. He took me to dinner and gently told me that none of the folks who held my current job was being considered seriously for a promotion, even though there were two open spots with a potential third opening. He came to tell me personally to soften the blow. He also assured me that if I did not get selected for one of the six positions, he would advocate on my behalf and look out for me. He was not concerned about my future and assured me that I had nothing to worry about.

I remember leaving dinner that evening. I loved the guy and considered him a friend as well as a colleague. I knew he was trying to help, but I was mad. I called him the next morning and thanked him for dinner. I also told him that I was going after my dreams. I would put my full weight and drive behind what I wanted. *I was going to make them deny me.* If, at the end of the day, my quest was not good enough, I could live with knowing I had tried my best.

Separation comes from preparation.
—Russell Wilson

I threw myself into the process of preparing. I have always been a voracious reader, so I quickly read three books on interview preparation and résumé writing. I created a book of Salisa that I would take through the interview cycle with me to showcase what I had done and what I could do. I answered every practice question in the interview preparation books and thought about additional potential questions. I also highlighted traits and accomplishments that I wanted to make sure I weaved into the discussions. I was so prepared that after the first panel interview, there was literally applause as the panel interview came to a close. One of my favorite sales coaches, Don Connelly, always says, "Successful people do things unsuccessful people aren't willing to do." This is another truth of mine.

I did get the job. Be careful what you wish for, because it might just come true. This experience taught me to go after what I really want in life. The worst thing they could have said to me was no. I put all the juice I had into going after what I wanted. Carla Harris says it best in her book *Strategize to Win*: "Fear has no place in your success equation; anytime that you operate from a position of fear, you will ALWAYS under penetrate that opportunity" (C. Harris 2014, 2339). I share this example because if I can go after my dreams and make them happen, so can you. I exerted an element of control over a situation that felt out of my control. I took control over what I can control, and that was me. I also used my secret weapon: mental toughness. Being mentally tough is something that I learned and continue to work on daily on, of all things, my yoga mat.

There's a correlation between yoga and leadership, and it all starts with being mentally tough. Yoga and leadership are both about doing what you need to do, not just what feels good. Mental toughness means choosing the *hard right*, not the *easy wrong*, as my yoga teacher Gary Olson would say. Mental toughness is about how you think, or maybe more accurately, it's about learning to stop thinking so much. As you will see oftentimes, thinking just hurts the team. I apply these lessons I have learned on my yoga mat in the boardroom in a corporate environment.

My sixteen years of practicing yoga have changed my life both personally and professionally. The life lessons I have learned have made me a better human being, wife, daughter, employee, leader, and team member. Yoga helps me be the best version of myself I can be. Yoga also challenges me to keep evolving. When you quit evolving and growing, you die. That may be a little dramatic, but when you fail to evolve, you definitely lose your relevancy.

Chapter 3: *Set Fire to the Rain*

I love the Adele song "Set Fire to the Rain." I set fire to the rain every time I walk into a hot yoga room. I have lived in Seattle since 1997. It's true that it does rain in Seattle a lot. I contend with the dark, dreary weather by stoking my internal fire with a hot power yoga practice. I show up on my mat and do my work. Once you learn to stoke your fire on your mat, you can learn to stoke and direct your fire everywhere, especially at work.

I have been in banking and financial services since 1989. I am sharing my experience as a leader and as a yogi because a lot of parallels arise where my two worlds collide. I understand that some people are not familiar with yoga terms or yoga postures, so please consult the "Resource Guide" at the back of the book for further tools or reading to learn more about yoga.

My yoga experience started back in 2001. I got hooked almost immediately. It's true that I started to learn yoga, but yoga is more about unlearning than learning. A lot of people think yoga is about the physical practice or the *asana*, or postures.

My yoga teacher Gary Olson has taught me that yoga is really about how you think—learning to control your mind. I was that gal who thought yoga and meditation were not for me. I had the original *monkey mind.* Marina Chetner says in her article "How to Tame Your Monkey Mind" that "Monkey Mind is a Buddhist term which describes the persistent churn of thoughts in the undisciplined mind" (Chetner 2012). What I have learned through my yoga journey is that yoga is for people exactly like me. Learning how to control my mind, slow down, and direct my thinking has been a transformative, empowering experience.

My nature is fast. I think fast, and I move fast; I even talk fast. This applies to my leadership style as well as my mat time. Through my yoga practice, I have learned to slow things down. This skill or tool is valuable in the corporate world. It's important to note this is learned, disciplined behavior. Let me share an example. I had a tough week. The stock market has been turbulent, and my team has been off their mark with their activities and results. My nature is to speed up, almost go into hypermode to get things back on track.

Hypermode is that high gear that you slide into when trying to grasp at straws to make things happen. It's that frenzied "just do more" state. You do more, or anything and everything, to try to drive better results. In my world, this could include a blitz, challenge, or contest to get things moving in the right direction. The better, more mature approach is grounded.

I have a great team. I need to slow everyone down and focus on the fundamental drivers of our business. Everyone needs to have a plan for what needs to get done that day, execute it, and follow through. The daily plan needs to include fundamental drivers, like how many calls need to be made, how many contacts need to happen, and how many appointments have to occur. An art and a science are involved in getting things done. The art is how you go about doing things; the science involves what you actually do. Going into hypermode involves what you do with an emphasis on just doing more. Going into hypermode can potentially have the exact opposite effect of what you intend. Going into hypermode holds the potential for letting folks get away from the very drivers they need to focus on to drive performance forward.

I am a good student of yoga and an even better student of leadership. The best leader I have ever worked with knew this instinctively. His job was to keep distractions to a minimum and help ensure I stayed on course with the drivers needed to move my business forward. It was like he put a pair of noise-canceling headphones on me to help keep outside noise away. He was a master at helping me stay clear on the best use of my time. He had a simple filter that we used to determine the best use of my time. I looked at the task or activity, and I asked myself if it would get me closer to my daily goal or further away from meeting my goal. Meeting face-to-face with a client who was going through a life-stage change almost always meant a good use of my time. Spending two hours of the day at a networking event or meeting may not have been what I needed to move my business forward that day.

We all have multiple activities and tasks that need to get

done. It all needs to get done, but he helped me organize my days to ensure that the critical activities got done first, with the *nice-to-dos* getting done at a later time or delegated to another member of my team. It was as simple as focusing on what was critically important to drive my business forward and pausing the rest. It's that simple. In the yoga room, Gary Olson always reminds us, "Just because it's simple doesn't mean it's easy."

The challenge is that it feels better to do something, anything, to move things forward. When you have uncertainty, it can feel right to go into hypermode. It takes a good deal of practice, intellectual honesty and discipline to stay the course. This is why a daily plan is so important. If you don't have a daily plan on what needs to get done, it can be tempting to say yes to everything you get asked to do.

I worked with a very talented individual. She struggled with results because she wouldn't say no to any opportunity to help people around her. We worked on defining what was the highest, best use of her time with the understanding that if she said yes to everything, it diluted her ability to be effective anywhere. This attention to detail had an immediate and profound impact on her results. She was immediately much happier because she took control over a situation that felt out of control and saw the results she knew she was capable of. Let me be clear; I can't always encourage my team to keep doing what they have always done, or we will always get what we have gotten in terms of results. The key here is recognizing the small, incremental changes with the biggest impact and when to take action on those incremental changes.

Chapter 4: *The Power of Process*

Routine, in an intelligent man, is a sign of ambition.

—W. H. Auden

One of my personal truths at work and in yoga is that I am a process-oriented individual. This is a good way to be. We need process in our lives. When we lack process, we need to work through even mundane experiences as exceptions. Think about something as simple as getting ready in the morning. I have a process that I use to get ready efficiently. I shower, blow-dry my hair, put on my makeup, and then style my hair. At home, this is an efficient process because everything has its place, and I follow the same routine to get ready. When I travel, the process is not as efficient because I am off my routine. I contend with this situation by putting a process in place in my hotel room to develop my new routine. It takes a day or so, but then my new process works as efficiently as the process I use at home. When I don't have a process, something as simple as getting ready in the morning takes more time and attention than it needs to.

This example illustrates my point. I picked up my car from the Lexus dealership. I had taken it in for service. When I picked the car up, someone had left the servicing checklist on the passenger seat. Lexus has a process, including a checklist, to ensure every detail gets tended to before releasing a car back to its owner. They don't make up the process each time. They have created a repeatable and sustainable process that everyone can follow. If something needs to be dealt with outside the process, then it is escalated. That is the power of process.

Operating without process is an extremely inefficient way to operate. In my world, this is the importance of having a daily plan for what needs to get done. If we take time to understand and articulate a process on what needs to get done that day, then we can go right back to process during times of uncertainty. If we are not clear about process, we become vulnerable to moving into hypermode, grabbing at straws in an effort to make things happen. That hyperactivity feels good in the moment, but we have to step back and examine if we are making progress or if we are drifting even further off target.

The key is slowing down and moving mindfully, deliberately—taking action, not reacting to everything around you. I learned this painful lesson in yoga and fight every day to apply the lesson at work. Moving deliberately takes discipline and focus. There are forces that will push you away from how you really should spend your time. Again, it can feel good to move at hyperspeed, but you really have to slow down and examine what is really getting done. Moving at hyperspeed often acts as a welcome distraction, doing anything but the hard work that really needs to happen to get things done or get things done right. Remember yoga and leadership are both about doing what needs to get done, not just what feels good in the moment.

A good example of this comes from my yoga mat with a vinyasa practice. *Vinyasa* means "to flow," so a vinyasa practice is meant to flow from one posture to another. When I first started doing yoga, I liked this approach because we would move quickly from one pose to the next. I was almost mesmerized by the movements; it was like a dance. However, as I built up strength and endurance, I came to appreciate that power and strength are really built in the long, controlled holds. If you don't believe me, go ahead and slide into a five-minute Utkatasana, or chair pose, or a five-minute Virabhadrasana II, or warrior 2 pose. You will quickly understand exactly what I am talking about. The untrained mind will pray to move and move quickly to something else.

I like to move quickly at work and on my mat. Nonetheless, I have learned that moving quickly oftentimes means glossing over a task or a pose. The real strength and mastery come in reaching the depth of a pose or the depth of a task and really seeing it through. This is why I strongly believe in working with a coach or teacher. I am strong in my mind and body, but I still benefit from having someone call me out regularly and challenge me to do more. This is true at work and with my yoga practice.

Action is movement with intelligence. The world is filled with movement. What the world needs is more conscious movement, more action.

—*B. K. S. Iyengar*

Making things happen requires clarity on what really needs to be done right now, understanding the highest, best use of your time in this moment. This is as much about knowing what to do as being willing to say no to things that you don't need to do now.

Chapter 5: *Slowing Down*

I was participating in a conversation about yoga at Smiling Dog Yoga in San Luis Obispo, California. Once a month, we would sit after class and talk about our experiences. A fellow yogi noted that you approach yoga as you live life. This rang true for me. Again, I walk fast; I talk fast. It's no mystery why I feel drawn to a very fast, athletic type of yoga. In fact, one of my former yoga teachers, Peter Avolio, used to call me Ballistic Salisa because I moved so fast. He always encouraged me to slow down. He would tell me I needed to slow down because if I didn't, I would get hurt.

Peter used to talk a lot in class. I like this from instructors as long as they have something interesting to say. Peter always encouraged me and my classmates to move more slowly, to move more mindfully. He went on to share that the slower you move, the more of life you take in. Think about this for a moment. When you fly to a destination, how much of the journey do you get to see and enjoy? How about when you travel by car? You get to see and enjoy more, but you are still moving fast.

I enjoy cycling. I like cycling because I don't spend a ton of time outside unless I am on my bike. When I travel on my bike, I get to enjoy more of the journey. I notice things that I otherwise wouldn't notice—a budding tree, the beautiful colors of the sky, the smell of the trees and flowers, and the simple songs birds in the trees that are singing to me. Think about the experiences you have when you walk or hike. One of the reasons this is so enjoyable is because you can take it all in. You can take in things that you otherwise miss when you cruise through life at top speed.

This same principle applies to things like cooking. Which do you enjoy more—a meal that someone special in your life thoughtfully prepared or something you grabbed from the pantry and heated up in the microwave? The same principle is true in yoga, and it's true in business as well.

When I was a new leader, I could easily feel overwhelmed by all the demands on me. I remember being in my office. My office phone was ringing, both my Blackberry and my cell phone were also ringing, and the pinging of my Outlook inbox sounded like a slot machine in Vegas! I quickly learned that I could turn the sound off on my computer and that I needed to minimize distractions so I could give 100 percent focus to the task ahead of me in that moment. Slowing down helps ensure that I see things through to the finish. That again helps me take control of a situation and ensures that I don't have one hundred projects that are midway through to completion. The key is slowing down and moving mindfully and deliberately.

Peter and my other yoga teachers had encouraged me to slow down for a number of years. In classic Salisa fashion, I didn't pay much attention to this advice until I had to. A couple of things changed my perspective. First, in May 2011, I was running down the stairs—ironically, on my way to a yoga class. I tripped and sprained my ankle and broke my right foot. The following year, I had a major surgery, unrelated to my foot injury. I had to take a six-week break from my yoga practice.

When I started practicing yoga again in 2011, coming back from my foot injury, I didn't pay much attention to what the doctor said. I paid for my poor decision making. My broken foot took longer to heal than it should have. I had a lot of pain and swelling for longer than needed because I simply wouldn't slow down and take care of myself. I should have given myself more time to heal, but I wouldn't stay off the foot. That experience served me well when I had my surgery in 2012.

As I came back from my surgery, I was careful not to harm my body. I was acutely aware of the fact that if I hurt myself or pushed myself too much, it would mean no more yoga for a long while. I simply had to slow down and take it easy. I had to take care of myself. What I learned from that experience is that when I slow down a little bit, I have the capacity to do more. When I slow down and take care of myself, I am stronger, with more stamina than I thought possible. Here I thought, as I got older, the process of working out, doing hot yoga or just physical exercise, was getting harder. I learned that I just needed to approach things differently.

This lesson was powerful for me. Less is really more. I can apply this back to work. When I was younger and inexperienced, I would write long, elaborate business plans. The more experience I've gotten under my belt, I have come to realize that less really is more. A great business plan takes this principle into account. Last year's business plan included my daily, weekly, and monthly to-dos. I had three to four to-dos for each time frame. As I mapped my plan out, it was important to me that I follow up on everything I committed to doing. In my world, you simply can't execute a million things brilliantly.

Less is really more in the workplace and in yoga. It all comes back to energy management. Less is more because everything takes some energy. I want to make sure I deploy my energy to the important elements or the vital few, not the trivial many. My energy is limited, so I need to work to make sure I do not waste any energy on unnecessary items, tasks, or movements.

This was really powerful for me. I learned that to do more, I needed to lighten up and relax a little. I was taking myself far too seriously. All I had to do was relax a little, and I could do more. It seemed counterintuitive, but it worked. It really all boiled down to learning to let go. This simple realization is true on my mat and even more relevant at work.

As I stated before, one of the great joys in my life is reading. I remember pretending to read before I could. I was so excited to learn to read. Even as a four- or five-year-old, I knew that learning to read would unlock a world of opportunities for me. I have been a lifelong reader and learner. I read about all sorts of people and topics. One of my favorite topics to read about is leadership. I enjoy learning about what makes successful people tick. I also enjoy reading about the approaches successful people have taken during tough times. Anyone can do well during good times. Great leaders shine when times get tough.

Back in 2008, I read *The Age of Turbulence* by Alan Greenspan. Alan Greenspan was one of the most influential, powerful figures in the global economy during the first twenty years of my career. I read his book interested to learn from his experiences. In it, he comments that there were times in his decision making that he wasn't certain what to do. In his words, "I don't pretend to know all the answers" (Greenspan 2007, 9). When Greenspan faced uncertain situations, he got very quiet; he watched and listened to everything and everyone around him. When he was quiet, he would get the information needed to take the right, deliberate course of action.

This was a powerful lesson for me. It was very liberating to hear Mr. Greenspan acknowledge that at times, he felt uncertain about what to do. Certainly, if he felt this way, it's perfectly reasonable that I acknowledge sometimes I feel the same way. The lesson here is when faced with uncertainty, you should slow down, listen, and watch what happens around you.

There is a tendency in corporate America to do more and do more quickly. Here is my truth. Sometimes, the best thing to do is slow down. Slow down, and do it right. Frenetic activity feels as if you are getting lots done, but I encourage you to really examine what you are doing. My truth is that when I take the time to quiet my mind, I am at my most creative and come up with my best ideas. I feel 100 percent confident that I come up with better ideas and I am more creative as a result of taking the time to quiet my mind. I see things more clearly and come up with solutions that are unclear when my mind whirls at a thousand miles an hour. I have to periodically step back, make and take time to quiet my mind, and just be. I don't do my best work when I constantly act and react to everything around me. This takes effort and discipline because things always come at me so quickly.

We face a lot of pressure to act and act quickly. Gary, my yoga teacher, loosely quotes Wyatt Earp on this subject: "Take your time, but take your time fast." What Wyatt Earp really said was "Fast is fine, but accuracy is final. In a gun fight … you need to take your time in a hurry." This is brilliant. Anything worth doing is worth doing right. Taking the time to get it right also reduces the time and energy devoted to rework. I hate rework. Take the time needed, and do it right the first time.

Chapter 6: *O Captain! My Captain!*

One of my favorite movies of all time is *Dead Poets Society* starring Robin Williams. I love the scene where the teacher, Mr. Keating, has just been asked to leave the school and his students, one by one, stand on their desks to pay their respects. They each repeat the line "O Captain! My Captain!" from a poem by Walt Whitman that they studied under Mr. Keating. It's such a moving scene. Every time I watch the scene, I can't hold the tears back. The students step up onto their desks to see things from a different perspective. My yoga mat does the same thing for me that the desks did for those students. I step onto my yoga mat, and I see things from a different perspective.

I strongly prefer to practice yoga after work. I am stronger and more flexible at that time, and frankly, I need the release after work. I literally go screaming under my breath to get to yoga. I hurry to get there, sometimes swearing profusely under my breath, doing my best to get there on time. I often laugh at the irony of this process. I stress out on my way to find my bliss.

I can feel stressed out and frustrated, trying to work through an issue, and then I step onto my mat. I leave all my problems and worries at the door. It never ceases to amaze me that after a simple one-hour sweat, I can see things so differently. I solve problems that seemed monumental just hours before. That's the power of seeing things from a different perspective.

Sometimes, I am too close to a problem or challenge I am trying to solve. Clarity occurs when I take the time to step back and see things from a different perspective. It feels as if I am looking at one of those pieces of art that you can't see up close. When you take a couple of steps back, you can see things more clearly that you couldn't make out when you observed them from too close up.

I love to be upside down. I was a dancer and an acrobat growing up. My mother teases me and says she didn't see my face for years. I would literally walk around our house on my hands, indoors and outside; I was always upside down. My family saw more of my bum than they did of my face. To this day, I love to be upside down. Although my meat-and-potato yoga is power yoga, I love yang yoga as well. I call it my *dessert yoga*. I do it just because it's fun. *Yang* (pronounced *yong*) is a playful style of yoga with lots of arm balances and inversions. It's a wonderful complement to my steady diet of power yoga and weight training.

I strongly feel taking the time to invert, or getting your legs above your heart on a regular basis, is the key to seeing things from a different perspective. One word of caution on this subject: If you are new to yoga, please be mindful when playing with yang-style classes. I am an experienced yogi with a ton of my life spent upside down. I have to watch my wrists and elbows. Too much yang is hard on my wrists and elbows. For that reason, I limit my yang practice to one or two times a week. The first rule of any yoga class that you take is do no harm. We practice yoga today so that we can practice again tomorrow, if we so choose.

When I feel stressed out or upset or I have a headache, my go-to solution is to stand on my head. Inversions energize the body. Being upside down is vital to my happiness and mental wellness. Inversions are touted as making you smarter. If you think it through, it makes sense. You bring freshly oxygenated blood to your brain from your heart.

My love of standing on my head is so strong that four days after I broke my foot, I asked my husband to spot me so I could move safely into my headstand during my home practice. He muttered under his breath, "Is this really necessary?" The answer was yes, I needed to get upside down to start to heal and feel well. Being able to see things from a different perspective is a vital leadership quality. Frankly, it takes effort and focus to not lose sight of the fact that you are a better leader when you have honed your ability to see issues and people from different perspectives.

I plan my weeks and calendar around my yoga practice. It's very much a way of life for me. To get the full benefits of yoga, you can't just do it casually or occasionally. I decide for weeks and months in advance when and where I will practice. I went to a leadership retreat and while taking the training was asked to prioritize areas of my life like family, wellness, and work. I prioritize yoga as vitally important to my well-being and my highest priority. My devotion to my yoga practice enhances my entire life and the quality of all my interpersonal relationships. I am 100 percent certain I would have killed someone or been killed already if I didn't show up on my mat on a regular basis and do my work. The world is not only a better place but also clearly a safer place when I practice yoga!

I enjoy taking classes. I'll practice at home or in my hotel room when I travel. I enjoy the company and energy of others. It takes a lot of energy to power my crazy, beautiful life. I have to take care of myself to lead and take care of others. I've learned this lesson the hard way. Since my life is planned around my yoga practice, that means sometimes when I am slated to practice yoga, I don't feel like it. Time is a big deal, or more appropriately, I don't have a lot of extra time in my life. Therefore, if I have time allocated for something like yoga, I have to go whether I feel like it or not. Even if I don't feel like going, I go.

Sometimes, it takes a lot of effort to drag my sorry self into that hot room and make myself move. I go and I do my work because it needs to be done. That is when I really love to be in class. At home, it's easier to give myself permission to lie on my back in Savasana, or corpse pose, for an hour and call it *yoga*. When I attend a class, I'm mindful of those around me. Sometimes, I share my energy with others around me, and sometimes, I need to borrow or share theirs.

I have a strong, fiery yoga practice. I love to practice next to strong, fiery people. That kind of energy feels masculine to me. This is a massive oversimplification, but a strong masculine energy is filled with strength, and a strong feminine energy is filled with more flexibility. Okay, I know folks reading this are getting ready to be upset with me. Please hear me out. I said this is a massive oversimplification, but it's true that different people have different energy. If you don't believe me, go to a yoga class, and stay mindful of the energy around you.

The reason I bring this up is that the perfect energy has a balance of strength and flexibility, yin and yang, male and female energy. It's all about balance. That's one of the greatest gifts yoga has given me—the gift of finding my balance. I don't always have it, but I know exactly where to go and how to find it. My favorite yoga teacher from California, Carolyn Sachs-Okonek, used to say, "It's available to you 24/7," once you know where to go to access your balance and find your peace.

I'm not really sure why, but I used to think I should've been born a boy. I felt as if my energy was more masculine. I realize today that I lean toward being stronger in my body (in my mind as well!) than being flexible. Professionally, I leaned toward an area of financial services that was male dominated. I also felt I identified more with the men at work than the women. Let me be clear. I always knew I was a female; I just didn't feel very feminine. At times, I wanted to be more feminine, but I didn't want to be seen as embracing being feminine. I would also go so far as to say that I felt embracing any femininity was a sign of weakness. I'm not sure where this came from, but this feeling was very real to me. I felt as if I needed to think and act more like a guy at work. Even in my personal life, this showed up. As a dancer and an acrobat, I was one of the stronger tumblers. That didn't seem very feminine to me. I'd watch the girls with slighter builds who were pretty and wish that I could be like them, but I felt different about myself.

I was also very competitive. I often stayed quiet about being competitive, but I always wanted to win at everything I did. I'm not saying that I'm the best at everything I've ever done, but I do have perfectionist tendencies that always make me want to be the best version I can be in whatever I do. As my good friend and leadership author Mark Crowley is fond of saying, "Any strength overused can at times become a weakness." I identify with his statement, noting that my normal attention to detail might be a strength in my business life, but that same tendency to be perfectionist can limit me and my willingness to try new and more challenging things in my personal life. So how do I win this inner battle? I remind myself that by getting involved with cycling or yoga, I'm growing and becoming more as a person. I started to win my inner battle by embracing one of the most important lessons or principles of yoga: acceptance. As long as I try my best, I need to accept that I am exactly where I should be, doing exactly what I need to do in this moment. I'll let some of my perfectionism go in order to maximize my own potential and give myself greater happiness in life.

I attacked the first part of my career with more strength, muscling my way through what I needed to do. Things started to change as a result. In my late twenties, a man who hired me helped me see things differently. His name was Shelley, short for Sheldon. I remember being twenty-nine years old and showing up for my job interview. I was moving from the bank side over to the brokerage side of the house. I went to my interview, and this short, Jewish man showed up. He had one of the biggest smiles I had ever seen. I did not expect a short, Jewish man with a big smile. That was the toughest interview I've ever had in my life. He really pushed me to see what I was made of. I clearly made the cut and got the job. I was hired as an assistant to a senior financial advisor. I did a good job, and eighteen months later, Shelley promoted me to financial advisor in my own right. He called me Roberts and treated me and the rest of his advisors as a team, not a collective of individual financial advisors.

I had a unique relationship with Shelley. He was my coach and sometimes acted like a father figure toward me. We connected on a deep level. He took the time to get to know me and really learn what made me tick. Shelley was one of those leaders who made me feel there was a giant safety net underneath me and I could do anything I set my mind to. At the same time, he challenged me and left me just insecure enough to keep raising my own lid. That's the mark of what great leaders and coaches do.

I had always felt inadequate. I think that will come as a surprise to those who know me, but it's an honest fact. I wished I had been born a boy and compensated for that fact by behaving in what I thought was a more masculine way. Shelley also gave me one more gift. In our many conversations over the years, he expressed to me how great it was that I was a girl. What a competitive advantage this was for me *and for him*. In fact, if he could find more people like me, he would hire them, but they are hard to find. We spent time talking about my soft skills, the things you can't teach people to do. They are innate in who I am—things like relating to people and caring and my approach to interpersonal relationships. You just can't teach people to care; people either care or don't care. I needed Shelley's validation to get in touch with who I really am and what I really am. Shelley's validation helped me get comfortable in my own skin. This was my first experience in bringing my authentic self to work.

The most successful people are comfortable in their own skin. They have come into their own power. You see, I had it all wrong. I thought embracing my femininity was a disadvantage. I learned this was really a competitive advantage—the yin and the yang, the strength and the flexibility. In her book *Power Yoga*, Beryl Bender Birch says, "Even iron will bend if you heat it up" (Birch 1995, p. 274). Just like iron or steel, I want to be strong, but I also want to be flexible in my body and my mind.

I am sharing my experience because this was powerful in my career and what happened next. Fully embracing all aspects of who and what I am had critical importance in helping me embrace my full potential. His moxie took some balls, but I'm so glad that he cared enough to share these things with me. As I slowly began to embrace who I am and what I am, good things started happening for me personally and professionally. Shelley was the first person, even before my yoga teachers, to teach me that using my whole brain and self was the ultimate competitive advantage. It is not just the brain and thinking; it is the heart and caring that are important. The former and the latter are both important, but the latter differentiates the good from the great.

Chapter 7: *Learning the Art of Relaxation*

I had been working through a tough time in my life. I've always been prone to waves of depression. This was a particularly tough wave, more like a storm of depression to navigate through. Depression feels like a dark blanket thrown over me. I've heard depression described by others as making you feel trapped down in a well. No matter how hard you try to get up and out, you feel as if you just sink further down in the muck. Depression is heavy and threatens to smother the life out of me. It mutes the quality of my life. Left to my own devices, I'd just crawl into bed, pull the covers over my head, and stay there all day. Being in bed is all that feels good when I am depressed. Unfortunately, I didn't have the luxury of staying in bed all day. I had to keep getting up and putting one foot in front of the other.

My therapist kept telling me that I needed to learn how to relax. My response was always the same; I simply didn't have time. Truth is, I didn't really know how to relax. I kept insisting that I slept a lot. My therapist continued to remind me that sleeping is different from relaxation. So, we went around this loop for a year and a half. Things really didn't change with my depression.

One thing that changed was my asserting control over food. I really stopped eating except the very minimum to keep me going—a welcome byproduct of asserting control over what I ate was that I lost nearly 30 pounds. No question I was overweight and could stand to lose a couple of pounds. Even at my biggest, which was probably 150 to 160 pounds, I still was not a big gal. I stand five foot four with an ideal weight of 128 to 130 pounds. The weight loss was welcome for me. I knew that when the wave of depression washed over me, I would go right back to my previous weight. I needed to make a change.

I had moved away from dancing and really any physical activity when I started my career in banking and financial services. During my twenties, my life was sedentary, with a couple of exceptions; no physical activity stuck with me. I was thirty now, though, and had just moved into my career as a financial advisor. It was a big job that required a lot of energy. I directed pretty much all the energy I had into my career.

Vanity helped me explore a Pilates class. After doing a little research about Pilates, it seemed like a good fit. I was really out of shape. I also had a lot of trouble with pain and popping in my hips. I wanted to try something to help me keep the weight off, and it needed to be low impact. That is how I made my way to the gym. I wandered into a Pilates class. I joined a gym right down the street from where I worked so I could take their Pilates class after work. In classic Salisa form, I just joined the gym. I knew if I paid money to the gym, I would go to my classes.

In reviewing the schedule, I noted a yoga class. It really was by chance that I wandered into my first yoga class. Yoga really didn't mean much to me at that time. It seemed to me that it had a lot of sitting around, chanting, "Ohm." That's not what I was looking for. Pilates was not offered every night, so I decided to check out the yoga class, simply because it was there and I was paying.

The impact of yoga on my life was and has been remarkable. From that very first vinyasa class, I was hooked. I have always been a big fan of vinyasa yoga, which just means that you flow from one pose to another. I remember that first class so well. It amazed me how hard it was to keep moving, but I loved it. It felt like an awakening in my mind and my body. The effects first showed themselves in my body. That first class hurt, but it hurt so good, if you know what I mean. It was that strange place that exists between pain and pleasure.

I have a classic type A personality. I'm a hard charging, driven individual. I didn't see yoga as a good fit for me. What I learned that first class was what a challenge yoga is, but when class was done, I was asked to lie still on my back in Savasana, or corpse pose. I felt a profound sense of calm in my mind and my body. When I got up from my mat, I felt longer, taller, and leaner. I wanted more of that feeling.

I had always considered myself an insomniac who sleeps a lot. Going to sleep has always been easy for me. Staying asleep is a different story. My monkey mind, like an Olympic athlete, just keeps running and jumping over endless hurdles. I felt at the mercy of my monkey mind, powerless to worry about the issue of the day. From that first class, however, I noted a difference in how my body reacted to sleep. I quickly fell asleep and stayed asleep. This is an understatement. I literally passed out from exhaustion and welcomed the restful peace and calm that come from the renewal. It was as if my mind quieted down to let me get the rest my mind and body needed.

I've always looked at good sleep like nature's candy. It just feels good. After I do yoga, especially a very physical class, sleep feels as if it pulls me under a current with water washing over me. It feels as if I am in a bathtub, when you sink down under the water and let it rush over you. I just surrender to sleep and rest.

The next day, I felt sore. Sore in the best of ways. Sore in my core. Clearly, my muscles had been worked. It was a great kind of soreness, though. I also moved better and felt grounded to the earth. I felt strong in my legs and across my shoulders. I immediately fell in love with this feeling. I loved the practice itself, how I felt during Savasana. I also noted a change in how I felt the next day. I was hooked. Yoga isn't just about how you feel during the practice. It's more about how you feel the other twenty-three hours of the day. For me, I feel well, grounded, and peaceful.

I experienced a couple of other welcome side effects. For example, I have to eat to practice the kind of yoga I practice. I have a strong, physical practice. I can't miss breakfast and lunch and expect to do my best on my mat. This quickly corrected my habit of working through lunch because I was so busy. It's a funny thing. When things are important or a priority to you, they get done. I must have protein during the day. When I fail to have protein during the day and then practice, my practice has a shakiness to it. I don't feel solid or grounded to the earth; I feel hollow. When I eat well, rest well, and have the proper hydration, I'm strong like an ox.

It was easy to fall in love with that powerful, strong feeling. I also feel my most powerful and sexiest when I am practicing yoga. I love glancing in the mirror and seeing the sweat pour off my curves. My muscles always look more defined with sweat cascading down everywhere. I love those feelings because they are internal and they are all for me. Prior to practicing yoga, I looked to the external world to make me feel powerful or sexy. It's satisfying that these feelings radiate from within to the outside.

I read a book by Dan Harris called *10% Happier*. Dan's book is great. He is witty and down-to-earth, my kind of guy. In his book, he talks about his relationship with meditation. He says it just makes him feel happier (D. Harris 2014). That's exactly how I feel about yoga. It makes me feel happier. It makes me feel well. I practice yoga for my mental wellness. I'm so lucky to have this wonderful tool to take care of myself.

In the weeks following my introduction to yoga, I started going more and more. First, I went once a week, then twice a week. Then I moved to three times a week. I have leveled off at four to five times a week. Yoga is a lifestyle. You don't get the full benefits from a casual practice. Again, it's classic Salisa. I don't do things halfway. I'm all in for the important things in my life.

I exited the relationship with my therapist about six weeks after I started doing yoga. I got what he was trying to teach me. I needed to learn how to relax. My learning here is that I didn't know what to do with the advice he gave me. I heard him tell me that I needed to learn to relax, but I didn't know what to do with that information. It was so simple once I found my way. This also underscores my point from earlier; you have to have the experience to understand the benefits. You can't sit on the couch and read *Yoga Journal* and expect to fully understand all the benefits of yoga. Yoga, like a good life, is experience based.

Over the weeks and months, I continued on my yoga journey. I'm not a mother, so I haven't experienced the joys of being pregnant. Pregnancy never appeared that joyful to me! I've heard women reflect back on that special time of their life. I know this seems crazy, but that is how I feel about those first days, weeks, and months of doing yoga. I always feel excited for someone who is new to yoga because I know all the wonderful gifts that are coming their way as they start their journey.

My body started to harden from the inside out. Oh yeah, that is one of the best benefits from my yoga practice. I got stronger both in mind and body. As I got physically stronger, I enjoyed my practice even more. My body got stronger, and I developed beautiful, strong shoulders. The dark cloud of depression also slowly started to break up above me. I felt like my life had been happening in black and white. Yoga helped me begin to bring color slowly back into my life.

I realize now that I was becoming more mindful. A mindful life is a happy life. I noted the beautiful blue of the sky, the autumnal colors of leaves changing, the crispness of the air in fall. All these things started to bring me joy. The changes didn't happen overnight, but they did happen. I also thought a lot about something my therapist talked about. I'm in control of my happiness. No one else can make me happy or unhappy. I was slowly on my road back to being happy. It felt great.

Chapter 8: *Being versus Doing*

I've always been attracted to yoga teachers whom I feel a connection with. I've been lucky to have had some terrific yoga teachers throughout my journey of learning yoga. I used to take a class from a gal who taught on Sundays. She'd tease that we were going to church. She meant it in a funny way, but I really enjoy a yoga teacher who has something meaningful to say.

One of the first things that I learned from Mary Thomas, my first yoga teacher, is that we are human beings, not human doings. This was profound for me. I am a doer. Actually, I am a doer in recovery because I recognize I can't do it all. A failure to accept this truth means burnout and heartache for me. In my personal life and my professional life, I feel better if I am doing something—anything.

Before I had yoga in my life, I'd do and do until I was sick and worn-out. I'd literally get sick and have to take a time-out to rest and relax. I'd emerge from this state weak, and the cycle would repeat itself. My therapist was trying to get me to understand that I needed to learn to relax. I repeat again that I didn't know what to do with that information. I slept; wasn't that enough? He saw the destructive cycle of working so hard that the universe stepped in and made me take a time-out by getting sick. The only thing that would make me feel better was downtime and rest and learning to take care of myself.

We need to give ourselves permission to just be without doing. This was profound for me. I was drawn to yoga for the physical expression. My mind and body loved a hot vinyasa class. It just felt good. I was becoming aware that all this working so hard was leading me somewhere. It led me to those precious few moments at the end of class in Savasana, or corpse pose. All I was expected to do was lie on my back and be. Now remember, I'm a doer, so this was super hard for me to do. Lie on my back and be? At first, I would break all the rules and multitask. I would review my day, create checklists for what I needed to do tomorrow, and wonder what was for dinner. You name it, I thought about it. I just didn't think that a quiet mind was for me.

I needed to be given permission to just be. I always felt the compulsive need to do something. I felt as if my value as a person or in the workplace came from what I was doing. It was refreshing to get permission to stop doing for a moment and just be. Clarity is found in the being, not the doing.

One of the reasons I love going to yoga is that no one expects anything of me in the yoga room. My cell phone doesn't ring. In fact, my yoga studio discourages my cell phone at all. No one can find me there! No one asks me a question and expects an answer.

For many years, I never said a word to anyone at the yoga studio except my instructor. It's my place to just be. I fiercely protect my special time on my mat. This is my time to take care of myself. This is also my time to receive. This is my time to feed my soul and take care of my body.

I had been doing yoga for three or four years when I got called to do something different in my career. When I was nineteen years old, First Interstate Bank hired me as a teller. I had worked my way up through the branch banking system. I'd always stayed on the sales side because I was good at it. When I was thirty, I successfully transitioned to financial advisor. That was all I ever wanted to do and be. I thought I was settling into a career as a financial advisor. It was a role I loved and I was good at. I loved helping people and putting them on the road to financial freedom. I'd made some errors along the way with my own finances, especially early in my life. I found making good financial decisions and helping others on their path to financial wellness very fulfilling. I looked at my role as my community outreach service.

I didn't realize how lucky I was so early in my career to have a wonderful mentor and advocate in Shelley Frank. Shelley hired me as an assistant to a financial advisor back in 1999. He eventually promoted me to financial advisor. We had a close working relationship. In late 2003, he came to me and talked with me about moving into a management role. I didn't know what to make of this idea at first. I had a successful career as an army of one. I liked working on my own and not having to depend on others. I also liked being in a position to speak my mind. I worried I was a little too mouthy for management.

I weighed my options very carefully. In the end, I decided to move forward. I was tentative, but I always knew I could pivot back into being a financial advisor again. It excited me to try something new and know I had a back-up plan with something I was really good at. I'd been a good financial advisor because I approached the role with the same zeal that I approach everything in life worth doing. I threw myself into becoming a great student of my industry. I read and learned everything that I could about what I was doing. I fearlessly approached my new role, always willing to try something new. Shelley had commented to me that the difference between me and others was that I was always willing to try something new and let it prove itself right or wrong. I agree with that assessment of me. I try new things to learn something constructive regardless of the outcome.

When I assumed my new role, I thought I was moving into management. I felt like a fish out of water. I had targeted becoming a financial advisor. I started as a licensed banker, moved into an assistant role, and eventually got promoted to financial advisor. This recent move was sudden and unexpected. I did what I always have done; I set about learning everything I could about being a manager.

I learned very quickly that my new role was more about leadership and less about management. My role had shifted; now, I had to get my work done through others. Leadership means getting people to do things they otherwise wouldn't do on their own. This is another parallel with yoga. We are good at the things we like to do and do most often. My yoga teacher Gary Olson likes to say, "We refine by doing." Yoga and good leadership involve doing what needs to be done, not just what feels good in the moment.

It's like your golf game. When I took golf lessons, my instructor said people show up again and again and work on their big golf swing or drive. They do this even though, statistically speaking, they would be better served working on their short game. Again, it just feels good to practice that big swing with the driver, so most of us focus on that if we don't have a good coach. A good coach makes us practice our putting and chipping. It takes mental toughness to work on what we really need to work on. Leadership, again, is about getting people to do the things that they otherwise wouldn't do on their own.

That first year, I read everything I could get my hands on regarding leadership. Years later, I would reflect back on my transition and note that I read twenty-plus books on leadership and management in the first fifteen to eighteen months in my new role. This was where I started to see the similarities between my roles as a leader and a yogi.

Chapter 9: *Using One's Intuition*

Lessons will be repeated until they are learned.

—Gary Olson

My name is Salisa; it rhymes with Melissa. This is how I always introduce myself. I love my name, but it's a hard one for people to pronounce. I have to assume they see it and give up. It's really not that hard. It's Salisa. It's not S*a*l*i*sa; it's not Cecelia, Falifa, Chris, or Salsa. My mother named me after a Russian fairy tale called Wassilissa the Beautiful (Williams and Dalphin, 1960). It's a wonderful story that I have read or had read to me countless times in my life. It's the same story my mother read or had read to her when she was a little girl.

When I was depressed, I wanted to spend a lot of time in bed. Spending all that time in bed led me to watch more television than usual. I remember Oprah Winfrey interviewing Caroline

Myss. Caroline Myss wrote a book called *Sacred Contracts* (Myss 2001). I don't recall a whole lot about that interview, but I remember my interpretation of her comments was that you need to learn certain lessons in life. The lessons will continue to present themselves over and over again until you learn what you need to learn to advance to the next lesson. I remember thinking that this episode was speaking to me. I knew I needed to read her book immediately.

We all have those moments in life when we don't know what to do. After reading this book and getting a better understanding of what Myss was saying, I understood clearly that at moments, I don't and won't know what to do. It's all right to throw my arms in the air and be open to what the universe is trying to teach me. If I am mindful and listen very closely, I can learn what I need to learn to advance on my journey. Here is the kicker, though; if I fail to learn what I need to learn, I can't advance to the next lesson or task. I will continue to be given the lesson or task again and again until I learn the lesson the universe is teaching me. This is how I grow, evolve, and stay relevant. Here is exactly what Caroline Myss says on this issue: "In short, a Sacred Contract is an agreement your soul makes before you are born. You promise to do certain things for yourself, for others, and for divine purposes. Part of the Contract requires that you discover what it is that you are meant to do. The Divine, in turn, promises to give you the guidance you need through your intuition, dreams, hunches, coincidences, and other indicators" (Myss 2001, 47).

The other powerful gift that I received from reading *Sacred Contracts* was a better understanding of my name's origin. Caroline Myss breaks down the meaning of the story. Dr. Clarissa Pinkola Estés wrote a book called *Women Who Run with the Wolves* (Estés 1992). Estés dates the tale back "even earlier than classical Greek mythology. (Myss 2001, 45). The story is about a beautiful young girl named Vasalisa. Vasalisa's mother is very ill. Right before her passing, she gives young Vasalisa a little doll. She tells her young daughter that whenever she's in doubt about what to do, all she needs to do is consult her doll. Her doll will help guide her to what she needs to do. Vasalisa's mother passes away. Like in many stories like this, Vasalisa's father remarries a woman who already has children, so Vasalisa now has stepsisters—evil stepsisters. The stepsisters are mean to Vasalisa and envy her beauty and kindness. They let fire burn out of their home. Vasalisa is sent deep into the forest to get fire from Baba Yaga.

Baba Yaga is a nasty old witch. She lives in a hut deep in the forest that is built on human legs. I would always picture in my mind this little hut running around the forest on little human legs. The witch gives young Vasalisa several impossible tasks to complete overnight before she will provide the fire requested. Vasalisa takes the little doll from the small pocket in her dress and asks the doll for help. Just as her mother promised, the little doll completes the impossible assigned tasks while Vasalisa is sleeping. Baba Yaga, the nasty witch, finally relents and provides Vasalisa with the fire she requested.

Caroline Myss breaks down the symbolism in her book. The little doll represents intuition, specifically intuition handed down from a mother to her daughter (Myss 2001). As I read about the meaning behind the story of my name, I felt deeply moved. My mother had given me a beautiful gift in my special and unique name. I had my own story. This also marked one of my first moments of awareness that I always know what to do. In the moments that I feel I don't know what to do, it's okay to throw my arms up in the air and ask for help.

Every time I have ever done this, my special doll or my intuition has guided me in the right direction. The key to this whole process is staying in tune with my intuition, being willing to listen, and not overthinking things. This was another one of those crossroads where my two worlds collided. We get so conditioned in business to think with the left side of our brain, the processor. It would take me a long time to figure it out, but all that thinking was the exact wrong thing to do. I simply needed to give myself permission to slip into a state of just being and let my intuition guide me.

Chapter 10: *Accessing the Inner Child*

I am the oldest child in my family, and for most of my life, I have been a people pleaser. That is the role I play and how I show up in most of my interpersonal relationships. When I started working with my therapist, he would ask me how I felt about things. It saddened me that I didn't know how to respond. I could easily respond regarding what I thought about different topics, but I didn't have answers when he asked me about my feelings on different issues. That was a sad time in my life. I was so out of balance and out of touch with myself that I couldn't determine how I felt about anything. How could I ever dare to believe I could get better? I just felt broken.

Looking back, I can trace where this behavior started. When I was seven or eight, my mom got her second divorce. Truth be told, I felt glad she was getting a divorce. I knew life would be better or less chaotic without her second husband. Even at the tender age of seven or eight, this was my truth. I remember when the divorce was completed, I stopped and thought about what it felt like. I stuffed what it felt like down inside me. I didn't process what I felt. I remember that moment clearly. I told myself everything was fine. I told myself I didn't feel any different than I had the day before.

I finally learned through yoga you have to process this stuff. You can't keep it all buried down deep inside you and expect to feel happy. My truth is that I have to feel to heal. If I don't process my feelings, it creates a toxic environment for me to live in, in both my mind and body.

I felt almost immune to feelings. I had stuffed my feelings about issues so far down into myself that I could no longer access them. No wonder I was depressed. I do remember a time when I could feel, but it was a long time ago. That's where my therapist went. We went back in time to when I could remember how I felt about things. In classic therapist speak, he asked me to get in touch with my inner child. I was such an ornery patient. This one almost put me over the edge. I didn't know how to go about this, and even trying was laughable.

This pretty much illustrates how my relationship with my therapist worked. We would talk about all sorts of things, and he would make suggestions. I would reject the suggestions or push back at first. Then I would leave and think about what we talked about. I was depressed and wanted to get better. I just felt unwell and broken.

I did try antidepressants for a very brief period of time. I did this because I had suicidal thoughts. I was scared of my own thoughts. I needed that to stop. I also wanted to be able to sleep. Sleep had always been an important part of my life. Now, nighttime scared me because my mind would run wild and out of control.

I very quickly threw my antidepressants away. They made me feel even more muted. I felt as if I was thinking in mud. The last straw was when I sat at my desk at work and felt as if I was drooling and couldn't think clearly. I threw the meds away and was 100 percent confident that I really wanted to feel what I went through, good or bad. A numbing agent wouldn't do anything to help me get better. I did think a lot about my inner child. I felt sad for her, but I had no clue how to access her. I didn't even know where to start.

I kept showing up and doing my work on my mat. I had started to do yoga. Almost immediately, I felt better. My body felt better, and after class, I would almost pass out and get that deep, refreshing sleep my body and mind craved. My body loved the experience. I got stronger every day. It empowered me to see the changes from class to class. My mind liked the experience as well. I began to have moments where I didn't think as much. Those were welcome respites.

I very vividly remember showing up and working very hard at class. As the class came to a close, we moved into Savasana, or corpse pose. I remember lying there and being able to just be, not think. It was a welcome respite to just lie there and be—nothing to do in the moment, nothing to worry about. Then we rolled over onto our right sides and curled up in a fetal position. In that transition, I found a connection with my former self, my inner child. I felt happy and content in that moment, connected with the happy little seven- or eight-year-old I had once been.

This was not something I tried to make happen. I just let go, and the powerful connection between myself and my former self occurred. It seemed to build an instant bridge from myself to myself. It created a healing moment, and I instantly became a believer in the connection to one's inner child. In that moment, I also understood exactly what my therapist had tried to help me discover. If I could connect with my inner child, I could make peace with failing to process the feelings I had stuffed down deep inside me. I needed that peace so I could release myself from the pain it caused me; it's a funny thing I learned this lesson. It was so powerful that I knew I was on the mend. It helped me build confidence that I could get better and that I was getting better. I never went back to my therapist again, but I did up my interest in my yoga practice and all the benefits. I slowly started to feel well again.

Chapter 11: *Creating Space*

Only in growth, reform, and change, paradoxically enough, is true security to be found.

—Anne Morrow Lindbergh

One of my favorite yoga lessons involves how to create space. I became aware of creating space in yoga, and I practice the concept at work on a regular basis. It can be best illustrated with an example. Here is what I would like you to do; sit down on the floor with your legs out in front of you. If you are like me, you will want to move the flesh under your bum away to the sides. You'll want to sit up tall, right on your sit bones. Your legs go straight out in front of you. When my legs are really straight, my knees kind of pop up off the floor. That's fine. Pull your toes back toward your nose so your feet flex. This sets you up for a pose called *Paschimottanasana*, or intense seated forward fold.

Now, you want to be careful here because you probably aren't warmed up. Lean out over your legs, and try to touch your toes. If you can, great; if you cannot, that's great as well. My former yoga teacher Carolyn Sachs-Okonek would tease us during class that if we could touch our toes, it was because we were enlightened. She was always careful to tease that if we couldn't touch our toes, we were also enlightened.

Back to the example! Be mindful of rounding your back. It's easy to round your back and get your nose to your knees. That's what you want to avoid. That will just give you a false sense of flexibility. You want to lean out over your legs, as if closing an overstuffed suitcase. You want to fold your tummy and belly button down first, with your head being the last part to touch, if that is accessible to you. It doesn't matter how far down you go.

If you are like most people, you will get to a point of discomfort. I have tight hamstrings, so this pose is a challenge for me. I fold forward, grab my feet, and immediately feel discomfort. When I hit the point of discomfort, I pause. Now, this is important, because this is what yoga is all about. Yoga is about how you think, not the asana or the physical practice. When you reach that moment of discomfort, I want you to pause before you do anything more. The intentional pause is important. If you are like most people, you either let your ego take over, round your back, and bury your face in your knees or worse—you snap out of the pose because it hurts.

I think of my muscles as giant rubber bands. Think about a rubber band in your hand. When you stretch it gently, the

rubber band lengthens. You have to be careful and mindful because if you don't pay attention, you can overstretch a rubber
band. Even worse, if you don't stay careful and mindful, you
can snap the rubber band. Your muscles are the same way. If
you pause when you hit that moment of discomfort, then you can
determine your next steps. If you learn to pause and be mindful,
you will lengthen the muscles and create additional space. This
is an incredible tool to have.

Gary Olson reminds me on a regular basis that yoga is about
creating space in your body and ultimately in your mind. The
more I practice this process, the more space I create. My body
and mind start to remember; I start to build muscle memory. I
hope this excites you, because this was huge for me in yoga and
even more powerful in the business world.

Here is how I apply creating space in the workplace. I have
a lot of different activities and tasks to manage and balance at
work. It's easy to feel overwhelmed by the magnitude of trying
to get everything done. The key to this whole process is the intentional pause. I pause and consider the highest, best use of my
time; then I create the space needed to do that and get it done.
The beauty of this whole process is 100 percent of the time, the
pause slows me down and gets me on the right track to focus on
what is the highest, best use of my time right then and there.
I never look back and regret how I used my time when I have
spent time on the most important tasks. This process helps me
take control of a chaotic situation and take mindful, deliberate
next steps.

Another opportunity to apply creating space is when dealing with a task or situation that seems hopeless or only has one potential outcome. The first step is the intentional pause. The second step is to stay with the situation for a moment and explore the outcome from several different angles. This approach often yields other potential outcomes that were not self-evident initially.

Our intense seated forward fold is a great example of the relationship between pain and pleasure. The untrained mind reads the discomfort as pain and wants to retreat. In this situation, no evolution happens. The trained mind notes the discomfort, or dis-ease, but stays with it and creates space, and then you can safely move more deeply into the pose. That's where the change slowly begins to happen. This is also what I love about yoga. You always have somewhere new to go. That's why it's called a *yoga practice*. You never master yoga; the work is never done.

Let me explain all of this another way. The discomfort you feel is your edge. We all have an edge in nearly every pose that we do. We all have an edge, maybe several edges in our personal life and in business. Your edge is that point where you experience resistance. The trained mind learns not to just retreat. In yoga, that means when you start to feel that dull, throbbing pain, you stay with it. If you practice this discomfort enough, you can reframe the experience and sometimes turn the dis-ease into ease, maybe even pleasure. You start to create space where there seemingly was no space. Stay with the dis-ease, and you can replace it with ease. According to an article titled "Why Disease? What

Is It? Where Does It Come From?" Sadhguru says, "The word 'disease', if you look at it more closely, is dis-ease. You are not at ease. Your body does not know how to rest" (Sadhguru 2008).

Let's go back to the intense seated forward fold example. This is your edge when you feel discomfort. If you can train your mind, when you get to that point, you can surf your edge. The edge and beyond are where all the good stuff is! You have to stay in the moment to notice this edge. Self-awareness is the key because this could be a dangerous place if you do not remain self-aware and mindful. This is where injury happens. If you have gotten hurt doing yoga, it's likely you didn't pay close enough attention to what your body was telling you. If your mind is quiet enough, your body will tell you what to do. Now, how do you get your mind quiet? That is another story we will tackle another time. Bottom line: Learn to surf your edge. When you find your edge, then you can start to push it out further! This is how you start to create space and come into your true power.

I apply this same principle in a business setting. I have done what I do for a long time. When I get to a point of resistance in my own mind, I pause, make space, and try to shift perspective. I have lightened up over the years on how some processes are managed in the workplace. Just because things have been done one way in the past doesn't mean they need to be done that way in the future. The whole process starts with the intentional pause and then an assessment to determine if we need to again follow what we have done in the past or if we have room to come to a different outcome to serve the situation at hand.

When I work through these situations, I am aware that I am dealing with an edge, maybe even a sharp edge. It's easy to be resistant, but it is hard to stay with it and see things differently. My ability to surf my edge ultimately will determine how far I soar in my life and career and how far you soar. Again, once you find your edge, you can begin to reshape your edges. That is how you evolve, grow, and stay relevant. For me, I use my hot yoga practice to continually shape, soften, and redefine my edges. The softening of my edges has been a softening process for me internally. Part of my internal dialogue after my intentional pause involves asking myself if I want to be right about something or if I really want to work through the issue at hand. This has been a letting-go process for me. In the process of letting go, I have found myself better able to collaborate with the people around me. If I give a little in the areas where I can, it allows us all to win. The process also allows the people around me to have better buy-in and more receptivity in working through future endeavors.

I had a former colleague who asked me for feedback on how he could more effectively communicate. I told him that sometimes when he tried to get his point across to people, he was so direct that it was painful to the folks hearing his message. They were immediately turned off and not receptive to his message. They walked away from their interactions with him feeling that his words had hurt them. Remember, people don't remember the words you used; they remember how you made them feel. He worked to soften his edges and his messages and went on to have tremendous career success before retiring. He struck the perfect balance of hard and soft.

The softening of my edges has contributed more happiness to my life. My softening has allowed me to coexist and collaborate more effectively with people who are different than I am. This has helped me grow more effective personally and professionally. I benefit from working with people who are different than I am. Diversity of thought is a great way to work through tough challenges. It has taken me a long time to realize there's more than one way to work through challenges and opportunities. It doesn't always have to be my way; in fact, when I'm open to other ways, often the end product turns out far greater than what I would have come up with on my own.

It's important to make time to create space. This is also a mindful process. I take four weeks off a year. I do this on purpose because I spend a good deal of my time very close to the action. When I'm so close to the action, I often react to what happens around me. When I react, I don't do my best work. My best work is proactive and all about deliberate, skillful action, not reaction to events around me. My time away is my cherished time. My mind begins to quiet down. When my mind is quiet, I am at my most creative. Stepping away and creating space allows me to step back into my role as a leader and do a better job.

When I read the book *Essentialism: The Disciplined Pursuit of Less* by Greg McKeown, it validated my feelings on taking time away and creating space, reading that Bill Gates regularly used "think weeks" even at the height of Microsoft's success

(McKeown 2014). The two weeks a year that he took as a think week were designed for thinking and reading. I do a much better job in my role as a leader and manager when I have time away to quiet my mind, think, read, and plan to charge the mountain. If this approach is good enough for Bill Gates, it certainly is good enough for me.

One of my favorite quotes of all time comes from a book called *Execution: The Discipline of Getting Things Done.* Authors Larry Bossidy and Ram Charan say, "People who can't work together reduce the capacity of their organizations" (Bossidy and Charan 2002, 127). My truth is that it doesn't matter how amazing you are on your own if you can't work successfully with others. You put a lid on your own success. Let this be a warning to anyone out there who digs his or her heels in and says, "This is just the way I am." I'm here to offer that you'll be richly rewarded if you willingly do the hard work of softening your edges. You will work more effectively with people and find yourself happier doing so.

Chapter 12: *Being Mindful*

One of the reasons I decided to write this book was to share my experience of being mindful. Early in my career, I didn't know what I didn't know. Then came the tough part, where you do the real work. The question on my mind was this: How do you know when to listen to your experience or when you are just being negative as a leader?

The truth is now I have a lot of experience under my belt. As I have new ideas and concepts shared with me, it's easy to discount them quickly based on my previous experience. This is where it gets tricky. I need to make sure I use my experience as a guide to make skillful decisions but stay open-minded enough to recognize when and how I need to make incremental changes. This has become hard as I've matured due to my work's demands, along with my experience.

My experience tells me that history doesn't repeat itself exactly, but it usually gets awfully close. The answer to this puzzle is being mindful. That's the only way to know if it makes sense to listen to your experience or to be open and willing to try something new. Timing and opportunity have to be in perfect sync for an idea or fresh approach to succeed. Going back to the well of previous approaches may seem the perfect solution today because timing and opportunity were off during previous attempts.

If you're like me, you get to moving really fast. Sometimes, I almost feel that I get into hypermode. This feels good, but I find that I become very reactionary when in this mode. When I make time to step away to think and plan, I make better decisions. A big part of this is the ability to see the big picture. When I am in that reactionary mode, I react and make small decisions that might not be the best long-term decisions. This whole process takes practice and discipline. For me, one of the best things about adulthood is making better decisions. I no longer have to live with the consequences of my poor decision making that sometimes plagued me in my youth. I find the same thing in business. The more care and time I take to make the right decisions, the less time I have to spend dealing with the consequences of poor or uninformed decision making.

A Reuters article validates my feelings on this issue. Titled "Market Yogis: Financial Planners Take Up Yoga," it says, "From many studies we know that mindfulness improves our attention to detail and ability to concentrate." The article goes on to say, "Research also shows that if you delay your decision making by even just a few seconds, those decisions tend to be much more accurate" (Reuters 2016).

Chapter 13: *Fall Seven, Rise Eight*

One of my favorite yoga teachers was Peter Avolio. One of the best lessons I learned from Peter was that my yoga mat is a mirror reflection. My yoga mat doesn't lie. My yoga mat knows if I've had the proper nutrition. My yoga mat knows if I've had the proper rest and recovery. My yoga mat knows if I've had the proper and required hydration. My yoga mat tells the truth and reflects what goes on inside me. I can't lie to it. All those truths or untruths come out on my mat.

Peter also used to say that if you want to be a better person, start by hanging out with a better version of yourself. Take care of yourself. Get the rest your mind and body need. Feed your body nutritious food. The single biggest thing you can do to improve your health and how you feel is staying hydrated. All the systems of my body work better with proper hydration. I feel better, and I look better. My skin looks better. I think more clearly when my brain has the water it needs. My elimination system works better. Water is my miracle drug. Once you realize the benefits of getting the water your body needs to function properly, there is no going back. The first stage of dehydration is fatigue. If you don't get the water your mind and body need, you should change this starting today. The change will help you on your yoga mat and help you stay more clear-headed at work and in life.

The power plant doesn't have energy, it generates energy.

—Brendon Burchard

My yoga studio is getting ready to expand. It started around 2004 with a main studio in Kirkland, and a second studio is opening in Bellevue. I was asked what makes my yoga studio special and why I go there. The answer is simple. Yoga helps me be mentally well. Yoga is the single most important thing in my life because the energy I create by doing yoga fuels my mental wellness. That might sound a little crazy to you, but my mental wellness powers my entire crazy, beautiful life. It takes a lot of energy to power my life. I have to take care of myself so that I have the capacity to take care of others. I know someone reading this thinks he or she doesn't have time to take care of him- or herself. You make time for what is important to you in life.

Some days, I feel selfish when I decide to take care of myself. When that happens, I think about the instructions you receive when you get ready to take off on an airline flight. The flight always begins with a safety demonstration. Do you know what they tell you about the oxygen mask when you travel with someone needing assistance? You need to put a mask on yourself first because you are in no condition to help others if you pass out and die. I think this is great advice, and I use it in a couple of different areas of my life. The first is with my approach to wellness; the second is with my approach to my finances. I take care of myself first so that I can take care of others. If I don't take care of myself, I am not in any condition to take care of others. I greatly enhance my capacity to care for others when I start with myself first.

My yoga practice is like a word processor—garbage in, garbage out. When I practice self-care, I see the benefits. The flip side of this is also true and even more important as I get older. If I don't eat right, don't get enough sleep, or fail to get the proper hydration, I feel it on my mat. This has another important correlation with business. You get out of your work what you put into it. So many people out there just aren't willing to do the hard work. They want all the benefits and glory but aren't willing to make the sacrifices or invest the effort needed. They lack perspective that hard work and effort are part of their growth plan.

This is an interesting conversation point because it boils down to intent and grit. Intent is hard to measure or gauge. As I contrast and compare successful individuals at work, in yoga, or frankly in anything in life worth doing, their success all boils down to their intent. The folks who succeed *intend to be successful*. They also have something special called *grit*. Angela Duckworth released a book called *Grit: The Power of Passion and Perseverance*. In her chapter on hope, Duckworth writes,

"Grit depends on a different kind of hope. It rests on the expectation that our own efforts can improve our future. *I have a feeling tomorrow will be better* is different from *I resolve to make tomorrow better.* The hope gritty people have has nothing to do with luck and everything to do with getting up again" (Duckworth 2016, 169).

Successful, gritty people make commitments, and they follow through on them. Gritty people don't give up; they keep getting up quickly after getting knocked down. The Japanese saying "Fall seven, rise eight" means to me that it doesn't matter how many times you get knocked down; what matters is that you get up and keep putting one foot in front of the other. People with grit are courageous and resilient. If you think back to the earlier conversation about self-motivation, you will recall Charles Duhigg indicates that feeling you can affect the outcomes of your situation is critical to improving your self-motivation. Moderately or mildly successful folks just go through the motions, ticking boxes. They just dial their effort in. They lack being present with the intention to succeed. They lack grit.

Through my yoga practice, I have learned to direct my intention where I want it to go. Directing my intention helps keep me in check and ensures I never feel like a victim of circumstances beyond my control. It's up to me to make things happen in my life. I'm 100 percent in control of the good and bad things that happen to me, or at least how I respond to the world and things that happen around me.

The drive to succeed comes from within. It's not an external experience. This is true in yoga but even more so in the corporate world. When I hire someone, I know almost instantly if he or she will have success. I can tell this because the good ones jump right in and figure things out. They exert the effort needed to help themselves. As my buddy and former boss Jay Coon is fond of reminding me, "If it is to be, it's up to me."

In reality, too many people look to others to make things happen. They whine about needing more coaching, training, and so on. The simple fact of the matter is I can trace my career success back to jumping in and figuring out how to make things happen. I have learned to problem solve in every role I have ever had. My experience and confidence have grown in every role as a result of rolling my sleeves up and figuring things out. This, coupled with ownership of both the good and bad outcomes, is the recipe for success.

Chapter 14: *When the Student Is Ready, the Teacher Appears*

My life and my schedule are busy. I show up to yoga classes because their time works for me. Truth be told, I am also a teacher stalker. Whenever people ask me for advice about yoga or starting yoga, I always encourage them to find a teacher they love. A good teacher can make or break a great yoga experience, especially early in your yoga career. The good news here is that I have had more good yoga experiences and teachers than bad ones. So, if you look, you will find an experience and a teacher that work for you.

When I started yoga, I did it at a health club. The environment was casual and not hot. I would show up to the different classes with different teachers and stay open to the experience. As I started to explore experiences and teachers, I heard about Johanna. She had a reputation for being a tough teacher. I have to admit she intimidated me. I knew how hard yoga felt in my body already. I couldn't imagine what she might expect me to do. I decided to try out her class and make up my own mind.

Johanna would show up to class early and warm up. We would all just watch in wonder at her warm-up process. She was so beautiful to watch. She moved so gracefully. It seemed that her body could do anything. I started to take her classes and stalk her everywhere she taught.

Johanna was one of those special yoga teachers who take the time to talk about yoga. Once a month, our group would stay after class for a half an hour to an hour and share our experiences. We found the conversations so rewarding that we started going to her home on a regular basis to enjoy tea together and share our experiences. My relationship with Johanna was a little like my relationship with my mother when I was a little girl. I looked up to my mom. She was so beautiful and self-assured, a very feminine creature. I felt awkward and homely. I hoped to grow up to become as beautiful and as comfortable in my own skin as my mom. I felt like an ugly duckling, and Johanna was a beautiful swan.

I asked her once if there was anything her body couldn't do. She smiled beautifully at me and told me it wasn't her body that was so flexible; it was her mind. She told me that my body was fully capable of doing the exact same things that her very flexible and strong body could do. It was actually my mind that held me back. This was the first time I was exposed to the notion that yoga is more about how you think than the asana or physical expression. She explained that she had trained her mind to take her body places. Most people aren't willing to stay with the process and train their minds when it gets tough or hurts. Think back to the intense seated forward fold example. This validates what Johanna said. Over years and years of practice, she had trained her mind to stay with a pose, create space, and go deeper. This is powerful stuff.

Johanna was my primary yoga teacher for three years. In that time, I learned so much from her and grew to love her. She spent time talking with me about her practice and experience. In all our time together, she never told me her age. Her age didn't matter; I knew I wanted to be just like her when I grew up. She would do all these crazy things in class, and I loved every moment of it. I estimate that she was in her early sixties. She was in amazing shape. She had the body of a fit thirty-year-old.

I felt as if practicing yoga with Johanna was an investment in my mental health. Just by looking at me every day, she knew what I needed. She was a master at reading my energy. It devastated me when she announced she and her husband were moving back to San Francisco. I actually felt that my mental wellness was at stake. I didn't want to go to her going-away party because I was so emotional. But I felt I had to go and say thank you for all that she had given me. In the end, I did go, and I bawled like a baby. I remember sobbing uncontrollably. She took my red, hot, swollen face in her hands and told me I would be just fine but that I needed to stay on my yoga journey. I promised her I wouldn't stop. She, in turn, promised me that if I stayed on my yoga journey, I would find my way. And as quickly as that, my chapter in life closed on Johanna.

You've been there. It's tough when your doctor, hairdresser, or massage therapist takes a break or moves on. That feels awful. Part of your tribe is missing, and it takes time to close that hole. I believe that people move through your life for a reason. Sometimes, they come into your life for a moment, a day, or a season. We are all just ships passing.

Chapter 15: *Hot Yoga*

I knew I needed to start exploring. I had a very basic under-standing of yoga and the postures. I headed out and started to play with different styles, studios, and teachers. I asked around for recommendations on where to go and which classes to try. Johanna had encouraged me to try a heated yoga environment. At the health club, we used the *Ujjayi* breath, or the "breath of fire," to create our own heat. I used to start my yoga classes all bundled up and slowly lose layers throughout the practice. I wondered what it would be like to try a true hot yoga experience.

The main turnoff about hot yoga up to that point had been the smell. I figured it just had to smell really bad, with all those people in such close proximity sweating on one another. Also, I am a mild germophobe. The thought of someone sweating and getting it on me grossed me out. I would never know until I tried, so I decided to check out a class.

My first hot yoga experience took place in a Bikram class. I thought the people were crazy! It was so militant, and they chastised me for bringing my block and strap. At that time, I had my own props, so I didn't have to share with anyone. I knew it would be hot, and was it ever. It was stifling hot, and the air didn't move. I felt sure I would pass out. I just wanted the darn thing over. I don't even know why I went back, but I'm sure glad I did.

I next tried a heated vinyasa, or power yoga class. I was hooked almost immediately. The room was a little sweatbox packed with people. The class was right up my alley. From the first power class I took, the whole group moved and flowed like one person. It was more like a dance than an asana. I also met my yoga teacher Gary Olson.

I felt at ease immediately when practicing with Gary. I felt as if he honored the work that I had done with Johanna with kind words and praise. He also took a sincere interest in my practice and pushed me, as he still does to this day, to work at my present level of perfection.

Have you heard the old adage "Practice makes perfect"? Well, Gary has a slightly different take: "Practice at your present level of perfection makes perfect." If you think about this, it makes sense. Gary says, "Your subconscious has no sense of humor." If you practice in a half-assed way, you refine a half-assed practice. This translates well at work. If you go about your work activities in a half-assed manner, you get a half-assed result. That's why accountability is so important. It's important to have someone watching, observing, and coaching you. That person sees things in you both in the yoga room and in the boardroom that maybe you don't see for yourself. I am driven, but I still need a little push or encouragement sometimes. There are days when I don't feel at my best. Gary won't have it. He wants me to either give my best or rest.

Through my practice of yoga, I have learned to listen to my body. When Gary pushes, I push back. He pushes me for more, to put in the effort required, and I respond by going deeper and giving 100 percent. This relationship works well for both of us. Sometimes, though, I need to lie out. So, now that's what I do. I lie down and close my eyes and surrender. It's taken me sixteen years to get to this point. The decision to struggle in the yoga room is simple. If you do struggle, you don't get the maximum benefit. The exercise gets to the point where you don't struggle at all. In the early days, struggle was part of my process. But I kept at it; I muscled my way through.

One day, I had a particularly fiery practice. When class was over, a new yogi approached me. She had been practicing next to me. She told me I had a beautiful practice. I smiled and told her I had years of practice. She asked me how I made it look so easy. She commented that I worked so hard but that she didn't hear a peep from me. I told her that it wasn't always this way. I worked really hard to make it look easy. Gary says, "That's the art of the art," working so hard that someone looking in thinks it looks easy.

I have to work hard to stay still or quiet. When I started taking a yin class, it was painful for my mind and body. The good news is that I have stuck with it, and the experience has gotten better for both my mind and body. The hallmark of a yin-style class is the focus on long holds to improve flexibility. I know better, but initially, I swore under my breath and just prayed for yin to end. Not a very zen-like experience.

When I lived in California, I had lots of different kinds of yoga experiences. I have always had a strong preference for classes where constant movement mesmerizes me. Those classes were my first stops on my journey back into myself. I would find myself lost in time and space, just being. My mind started to quiet. My mind wasn't quiet all the time, but I started to experience moments of quiet. I started enjoying moments where I just was being, not doing anything. When I slid back into my real life afterward, I felt so much better—dare I say *normal,* whatever that is.

Chapter 16: *The Long Road Back*

In June 2012, in a sudden and unexpected manner, I found out I needed major surgery. My right ovary was a mess and needed to come out immediately. A concern came up that I could have ovarian cancer. I had some other issues then too, so it was an easy decision for me to have a hysterectomy at the same time. Lucky for me, I was a good candidate for the robotic surgery. It was less invasive with a shorter recovery time. My goal through the whole process was to get healthy and return to my life and activities as quickly as possible.

That was a scary time for me. It was really the first time in my life that I questioned my own mortality. Years before, a friend of mine had lost her husband to surgery. He went in for a routine sinus surgery, developed a blood clot, and died that same day. I knew the odds of that happening to me were low, but I still faced a risk. I pushed myself hard in the days and weeks leading up to my surgery. My family commented that I could take it easy; I clearly had issues. No one would have questioned me slowing down and not pushing myself so hard. Pushing myself hard both at yoga and on my bike was my form of preparation. I knew the healthier my body and mind were prior to surgery, the quicker I would recover.

In the days and weeks leading up to my surgery, I directed my love, attention, and healing thoughts to my broken ovary and uterus. I lay in Savasana, placed my hands over my pelvic area, and directed my thoughts and attention to the broken area. At first, I directed my attention to my right ovary that was dying. I did switch gears and decided to focus on directing my attention and love to my healthy ovary that I wanted to keep. That was the first time I really thought about how and where I could direct my attention and energy. As I reflect back, this was where I started to play with the notion that I could direct my attention and intention in a certain direction and make things happen. Pretty powerful stuff. I was always careful to direct positive, healing thoughts to my broken parts.

It terrified me to be off work for a whole month. What would I do without my work that I loved and my yoga? The goal was clear. I needed to take good care of myself so that I could heal properly and get back to my beautiful life. In my preparation for my surgery, I learned that I could walk following surgery. That would get me moving as quickly as possible.

I came through the surgery with flying colors—no cancer, no complications, thank goodness. However, I did have a challenge to my coping skills. My beloved cat Bailey died the same day I came home from the hospital. I didn't have the capacity to deal with Bailey's passing at the time. I had no energy, not even enough energy to cry. All I wanted to do was sleep.

Every day, I made myself get up and go for a little walk. I expected that I would better my best a little every day. It felt so strange to have been so strong and then feel so fragile and weak. I started slow by walking out to get the mail and beyond. It was crazy how mild inclines in the pavement would wear me out.

I have always been a sleeper, but I impressed Mark by taking three to four naps a day during that time. I indulged every want to sleep and rest. I heard Gary's voice inside my head, saying, "A relaxed body receives benefit." I did my very best to keep my mind and body relaxed. It was interesting to see how incapably I dealt with stress during that time. I would quickly feel overwhelmed and burst into tears. I didn't even want to make small decisions, like what to have for dinner. I just wanted to walk a little, avoid stress, and sleep. I ate just enough to keep me going. I existed on cranberry-orange bagels with strawberry cream cheese and fruit. I hadn't really eaten or craved bagels and cream cheese prior to surgery. Mark and I would joke that I was pregnant—clearly not!

I did have to back off the walking because I was pushing it. The more I walked, the more I felt my insides might fall out. I finally relented and gave in to pure rest. Although I am not a doctor, I do realize that if something hurts, you need to stop doing it. This is interesting and relates to something else yoga has taught me—awareness. Not all pain is the same. A burning-hot, searing pain is bad. When you feel that discomfort, you need to back off. This is where people hurt themselves. A dull, throbbing pain is different.

I feel that kind of discomfort a lot in yoga. That dull, throbbing discomfort is the kind of sensation you want to stay with and then create space and go further. Making the distinction takes discipline and awareness. The untrained mind pulls back and away from any discomfort. I have loved learning to stay with that dull, achy discomfort and deal with the dis-ease. I firmly believe that I ward off disease in my body this way.

I went back to work on time, thanks to the terrific team around me. Mark; my boss, Jay; my amazing assistant, Heather; and the team of people around me were great. Everyone was watchful and helpful, making sure I didn't overdo it. I gave myself permission to rest and recover. I did this because I aimed to get back to my full life as quickly as possible. The doctor instructed me to do no exercise or physical activity for six weeks. Then he said I could slowly ease back but I had to be careful. I also remember him telling me that I needed to be careful twisting my insides, due to all the work that had been done. Getting back to twisting excited me, though, because I had had parts removed. It excited me to see how much more space I had to twist, with fewer parts.

A day before I was supposed to, I decided to return to yoga. The year before, I had broken my foot. I had practiced yoga at home the whole time because I just don't hold still well. Recovery from my surgery, however, was different from recovering from my broken foot. I tried to do some mild stretching at home, but I missed going to my yoga classes. My first class back took place on a Friday night. I picked Friday night because the classes were usually smaller then. I knew I could easily hide out in the back and not be self-conscious. It excited me to head back into the yoga room because I had lost weight and I knew I would look great in my new red yoga shorts.

I felt so glad to be back. I know this sounds crazy, but I missed The Ashram so much. I missed the smells and the sounds. Gary knew I had had a major surgery, but I had not shared any of the details. He was glad to see me and noted how good I looked. He only asked that I take care of myself. The first rule of yoga and the first rule at The Ashram is "do no harm." I felt acutely aware of the importance of doing no harm. It took all my energy just to get dressed and into the yoga room that night. I felt exhausted before I started. I made a commitment to myself to do no harm. If I messed up, I knew I may not come back for a long time. I know my decision to return so fast concerned Mark and my boss, Jay. I just had to do it. It was right. This was where I went to heal and get well. I couldn't really feel on my long journey back to health without yoga and The Ashram.

I remember lying on my back on my mat, just taking in the noises and smells of The Ashram. I had a sense of well-being. At that moment, I knew I was on my long road back to recovery. That evening still stands out as one of my best yoga classes ever. I couldn't do much, but I got so much out of it. I did the majority of the class on my knees. I rested almost the whole class.

About three-quarters of the way into the class, I was done. I lay on my back with my feet up the wall for the rest of the class.

Gary was supportive through the whole class and checked in with me a couple of times, reminding me to do no harm. I seldom just do what I want to do in the yoga room, and I appreciated that Gary gave me space to do my thing. My Savasana, or corpse pose, that evening was amazing. I was slowly making my way back to health. Every movement was deliberate and intentional and exercised with care and love.

In the days after that, my yoga practice became like an exploratory mission. All my ability was still there, but I had to find it one day and one pose at a time. It posed a great challenge for my ego. I always stayed mindful that if I hurt myself, it would set back my recovery.

In those days, I got another precious gift. I learned the importance of really moving mindfully. I found that when I moved more slowly, I could do more. "Ballistic Salisa" would move fast and tire herself out. When I timed my movements with my full breath cycle, I had the capacity to do more. I also didn't find myself winded. That's what the new yogi next to me admired. I moved mindfully, still powerfully but in total control. She commented that her breath was labored and she had not heard a peep from me.

I started to bring this same thought process to work with me as well. I moved more mindfully and intentionally. Sometimes, hyperactivity is good, but slow and intentional is even better. I learned that I have to make time and space to move more intentionally at work. It requires that I take regular time away to think and plan, then execute. The thinking and planning part should ideally take about a quarter of the time, with the other three-quarters of the time focused on execution. When I am too close to the action, without strategy, I can easily get sucked into the mode of reacting to everything around me.

I have suffered through the consequences of reacting to situations and making the wrong calls. One example of this is just agreeing to something a team member asked for without taking time to think through the request. Another example is hiring someone because I needed someone and not taking the time to ensure the person was the best fit for the role and organization. The mindful and intentional lessons here are to not agree to an ask until you have reviewed the issue and to take the necessary time to make sure additions to a team are the right fit.

Chapter 17: *Holding Space*

Fellow yogi Lena Hirschler shared her experience and thoughts on holding space. Holding space is a powerful tool that I use in the yoga room and in my personal life, and it serves me very well in the boardroom. I apply holding space by weighing a situation and not initially reacting. I let the situation unfold so that I can better understand what's going on and how I can skillfully intervene.

Let's start with an example involving the workplace. Part of my role as a leader is dispute resolution. I remember one of my first situations where I was charged with dispute resolution. Two people were not getting along, and my colleague and mentor and I were charged with getting this team back on track. I was a new leader at the time. During the long ride to visit one of the offending parties, my colleague asked me what approach I would take. I don't exactly recall my answer, but I can tell you I chose the wrong approach. I'm sure in my inexperience, I planned to let the guy have it and tell him how it should be.

My mentor reasoned that it was important to hear his side of the situation and reason with him. I needed to meet him where he was and help him self-discover the next steps. Looking back, I see my mentor meant that I needed to skillfully intervene, not make the situation worse. The best way to skillfully intervene is to observe without judgment and gain information and insight into the situation.

It never ceases to amaze me how differently people can react and respond to the same situation. Learning how to skillfully intervene really means stopping to hear what the other person says and then helping that person see the situation from the other one's perspective. Now, this doesn't always work, but my approach to listening and getting information and insight does work. It helps me understand where the person is coming from and then aids in crafting an approach to help him or her move forward. It's about meeting the person where he or she is and then bringing him or her along.

Here is how holding space helps in these types of situations. Many of these situations are emotionally charged. As a new leader, I would react to the first person who got to me due to my inexperience. I would get sucked into his or her interpretation of what was going on. The challenge with these situations is one person's perception of the situation is his or her truth, but the real truth lies somewhere between the two people's views of the situation. Multiple realities really exist. It's amazing how different a situation can appear when viewed through each participant's filter.

I have since learned that skillful intervention requires me to

hold space, or disengage from a situation's emotions, so I can observe the situation and gain insight into it. This approach requires
me to step back and listen to what is being said and perhaps what's
not being said. This approach helps me focus on the facts, not all
the emotions related to the situation. After I have held space and
gained information and insight, I can skillfully intervene to help
resolve the situation or at least move past the situation.

It doesn't work to get sucked into a situation and the associated drama, especially with the first person. Yoga has helped
me understand how to manage my energy. I only have so much
energy; it's up to me to decide how to use and direct my energy.
If I get sucked into drama-filled nonsense, then that is how I have
chosen to use my limited energy. In learning how to hold space or
detach, I can remove myself from the drama of these situations
and make better, more informed decisions. After I have gained
insight and perspective in a situation, then I can use my energy
in a positive manner to resolve the situation or move it forward.

I look at my energy as I look at my time. My energy and my
time are precious resources. With practice, I have learned how
to use them both wisely. Holding space is a great technique to
help me deploy my energy wisely. This life lesson has served me
so well on my mat and even better at my desk.

A word of caution for when you hold space: The holding
space technique frustrates the folks you work with as you apply
it. Whether they are upset team members or unhappy friends or
loved ones, they look for a reaction from you. When they don't
get the desired reaction, they don't find the game fun, and they

move on to other folks they can interact with who will feed their negative energy.

It's interesting to see how many people feel that a leader's job is just to tell others what to do. I understand that folks see that as an easy fix, but often, you have a more effective way to help. You can choose to lead with authority or influence. I strongly prefer to try to influence first before using authority. Most of the time, command and control don't work or stick. We have better ways to skillfully intervene than to just tell people what to do. The whole key to this process is that intentional pause before taking action to skillfully intervene. It all goes back to creating and holding space.

When Lena and I talked about holding space, I thought about it from my perspective, especially at work. When something happens to me that I need to work through, this is one of my techniques I use to manage my energy and deploy it wisely. Holding space goes so deep. It gives you an opportunity to really connect with other individuals, to help and support them as they move through their journeys and experience.

The leader in me always has a knee-jerk desire to jump in and start problem solving. Oftentimes, we can take a more effective approach. A skillful alternative is to be there for an individual. Listen to his or her perspective without judging or trying to fix the situation. Again, just be, and suppress the impulse to do or to move through the situation. This supported approach takes more time, but it allows the individual the time and space he or she needs to move through a tough time or situation.

Chapter 18: *Like Attracts Like*

It's interesting to stand back and observe interpersonal relationships and exchanges. One of Gary's main principles in yoga is that like attracts like. Here is what I mean by that. When I feel angry or upset, I interact with the world in an angry and upset manner. I get back more anger and frustration in return. You get back what you put out there. I am not perfect on this issue, but when my clearer head prevails and I keep my temper or fire under control, most of the time, my good behavior gets rewarded.

I pride myself in my ability to work with difficult people over the years. Part of my method of madness is to not respond to their bad behavior. When people are angry or frustrated and they come at you that way, they expect a response. When you hold your space and respond with kindness, most of the time, it softens even the hardest of people. I do not suggest this works all the time or even immediately, but it does work.

You get back what you put out there. People who reach out in a nasty way are conditioned to get back what they put out there because like attracts like. The approach of leading with kindness takes discipline and practice. I still have the same urge to react to poor behavior with negativity, but I find it more productive to take the higher road and be kind. If that still doesn't work, I 100 percent know I did everything I could to help. You know what they say; you can't help people who don't want to help themselves. Next time you get all worked up about something, note that if you respond with fire, you'll likely receive fire right back. I offer you have a better, more productive way.

I have often been asked how I avoid people wasting my time with complaining or whining. My best coping technique is that I practice holding space or detachment. It helps me not get sucked into the vortex of their drama. It also helps me be a happier person. The other technique I use is I reframe whatever issue the person complains about as what he or she could do to get a different outcome. This is a terrific stopper because I can tell when someone really wants to work through a problem and when one just wants to whine and cry about something. The people who want to whine and cry have no intention of doing anything different to help the situation. The ones who want to review a situation and better understand how they show up in the situation are the ones capable of change, evolution, and growth.

Remember what Charles Darwin is thought to have said: "It is not the strongest of the species that survives, nor the most intelligent that survives. It is the one that is most adaptable to change."

Chapter 19: *Show Up and Do Your Work*

I am the oldest child in my family. I come from humble beginnings. My siblings and I were not raised with a lot of material things. We had the important things in life. My mom still comments that she wishes she could have given us more. I feel grateful for how I was raised. I learned to work hard for what I want. I also learned to take good care of things.

In my role as a leader, I get asked for career advice on a regular basis. I always tell people to work hard and maximize every opportunity for improvement. A truth for me in my personal and professional lives is that the harder I work, the luckier I get. This applies to work and yoga. I feel old when I say this, but I see this with people today. When they come into the workforce, they want a role with power and respect. They don't want to start at the bottom. Often, they feel that because they went to college, some tasks or roles are beneath them. They are missing out. I started at the bottom and worked my way up. I learned everything I could about the different roles. That has hugely contributed to my success. I know every role on the ladder of success inside and out. I was willing to put in the hard work. I did what it took to succeed in every step on my career ladder. Each step was part of my overall growth plan.

My mom told me to take every job I got seriously and treat it with importance. I have always tried my hardest and given my best. That advice has served me well. I have approached every job or assignment as if my company or my boss couldn't exist without me. Others have come to see me the way I see myself. I have gotten assignments or tasks that would never have gone to me, but I showed up every day, gave my best, and asked those around me what I could do to help them.

In yoga, this advice has also served me well. When I quit dancing, around twenty or twenty-one, I moved into a sedentary lifestyle. All through my twenties, my lifestyle was sedentary. There were some exceptions, but I really got out of shape and gained extra weight. It intimidated me to start moving again because I had gotten so out of shape. I felt big, slow, and heavy. My ego got in the way of getting moving. I remembered what I used to be able to do. I found it hard to focus on what I could do or to not become frustrated by what I couldn't do on any given day. It took a lot of hard work to get my body and mind back into shape.

Yoga is about how you think, not the asana or the postures. It takes a lot of discipline to show up on your mat every day and do your work. A lot of people aren't willing to work that hard. It's easier just to sit on the couch. Here is a goodie from Gary that I picked up on my yoga mat that I use both in yoga and in corporate life: "Progress is based on where you were to where you are, not where you are to where you want to be." Truth! The former is the truth; the latter is an aspiration.

Another truth at work and in yoga is part of succeeding is just showing up every day! This sounds so easy, but it's true. This has been the number-one contributor to my career success. I show up every day and do my best. My job as a yoga student is also to show up every day and do my best. Now, my best varies from day to day, depending on how I feel.

Sometimes, I feel like a rock star. I go really hard, and I am as strong as an ox. Other times, I go into the yoga room, lie down, and don't want to get off the floor. My yoga is to stay on my mat and breathe. That's hard on the ego, but it's what my body and mind need that day. Gary says that my job is to show up. His job is to get me through class. Sometimes, I don't want to go do yoga; I show up, though, and get my work done. Oftentimes, I have the best classes when I least expect it. The inverse is also true. Sometimes, I show up at yoga feeling like a rock star and end up on the floor sucking wind for most of the class. The lesson here is you have no expectations on your mat. Show up every day, and do your work.

I strongly feel that how I think has been the secret sauce behind my career success. My career success directly relates to my will to win—my will to succeed. Skill certainly plays a part in the process, but you have to show up every day and give your best at anything important in your life. Remember, you get out of things what you put in. That principle applies to yoga, career success, and life in general.

Chapter 20: *Be Humble and Kind*

My husband and I enjoyed an evening out. We decided to go to a local comedy club. Jeff Dye, the comedian, was performing. Mark and I have loosely followed his career success. Watching the television show *Last Comic Standing* introduced us to Jeff and his comedy. I love witty, smart people who can think on their feet. If I boiled Jeff's message down to one important sound bite, it would say, "Be nice." Be nice! My mom told my siblings and me to be nice while growing up in my household. I have always wanted a bumper sticker that says, "Mean people suck."

Yoga contributes to my niceness. It makes me feel good in my body. When I feel good in my body, I feel good in my mind. I am convinced that a lot of people on this planet don't feel well in their minds and bodies, and it's evident in how we treat one another. I feel that yoga makes me dig deep into myself and pull out the best parts. It feels good to be open and receptive to the world and people around me. I'm also a constant work in progress, using my fire to soften and smooth my edges.

Here is another truth of mine. If you don't feel good in your mind, get your body moving. Reading Beryl Bender Birch's book *Power Yoga* underscored this point for me in a huge way. Birch writes, "The body and mind are inextricably linked—whether we like it or not. We can't just hope to control our mind and ignore the body. If the body is out of control (or out of shape or alignment) the mind cannot possibly be in control" (Birch 1995, p. 34). I interpret this to mean that to be right in your mind, you need to be right and healthy in your body. This is my personal truth. I have lived in an unhealthy body. Now, I work very hard to live in a healthy body. I tell you, it is better. Again, if your mind doesn't feel right, it makes sense that you may not be as nice to others around you as you should. I just feel well when I have the sense that I am taking care of myself. I know what it is like to feel mentally unwell, and well is better. I feel prouder of the person I am and prouder of the way I live my life when I am nice.

Tell me, what is it you plan to do with your one wild and precious life?

—Mary Oliver

Looking back, I am glad that I did work with a therapist. One of the biggest lessons I took away from that experience is I am in control of my happiness. Prior to working with the therapist, I was a good little martyr, and I looked to the external world to

find happiness. This was true in my personal life, my relationship with Mark, and my family and work.

The yoga experience has empowered me to do whatever I
seek to do in my beautiful life. I have learned to surf my edges,
knowing full well that everything good in life is hard and it takes
work and effort to get there. I am willing to put in the hard work
and go after what I want. It feels amazing to make this procla-
mation to the world: I am in charge of my happiness. I choose
to be happy.

Diana Schneider says, "Optimism is an intellectual choice,"
and she's right. This realization helped me set fire to the pain I
felt, looking to the external world for my happiness. It isn't that
the world or people around us don't care; they just have their
own stuff to deal with. I fundamentally believe that the vast majority of us are all just trying our very best. Living life with this
thought process means giving people the benefit of the doubt,
even when they are having a bad day.

I had a situation that really put all of this to the test at work.
The details of the interaction don't matter. What does matter
is an individual went off on me. She made personal accusations
about my company and me that were way off base. She came
at me in two different tirades. I proudly held my composure; I
held space. I bet my blood pressure and heart rate didn't even
rise. The negativity rolled off me like water off a duck's back. At
a different point in my career, I may have responded in a different manner, a manner that would not have been productive for
anyone.

When I finished the phone conversation, I paused. I felt sad for this individual because, clearly, something going on in her life made her lash out at someone sincerely trying to help her. I felt proud of myself that day because that conversation was a potential derailer. No one working through a similar situation would have blamed me if I got in a foul mood or let the interaction ruin my day. However, I chose to be happy.

I have 100 percent control of my happiness. That doesn't mean I don't have dark days in work and in life. My perspective on how I deal with these types of situations has changed. I want to be clear; this means seeing things from my chosen perspective and owning how I feel. It doesn't mean stuffing how I feel down and dealing with life in a Pollyanna-ish type of way.

In my late twenties, I spent a couple of years working in a corporate training department. It was a fun job that I really enjoyed. One of the simple things I used to teach people was to smile at others, especially unhappy people. Sometimes, a small acknowledgment can go a long way in helping another person feel you have recognized him or her. If you don't believe me, try it yourself. For the next day or so, smile at everyone you see. Most of the time, my smile is returned with a smile. This validates that I get back what I put out there. The flip side of this is if you walk around frowning or scowling, you will largely get that back in return.

Chapter 21: *The Man, the Myth, the Legend*

In April 2015, I received a phone call telling me that my favorite mentor and coach had passed away suddenly. Shelley woke up one morning, went to play tennis, and had a massive heart attack. The only peace I took in hearing this news was that he went fast. This news made me profoundly sad. Shelley had made such a huge dent in my life, and then he was gone. I took solace in the fact that I had taken the time to tell him how much his love and support had meant to me over the years. I am 100 percent certain that he knew how I felt about him and the wonderful imprint he made on me both as a person and as a professional.

Shelley believed in me. He believed in me at times when I didn't believe in myself. At times in working with Shelley, I put one foot in front of the other to keep going just so that I wouldn't disappoint him. Shelley saw things in me that I couldn't see in myself. He created an environment where I felt I had a giant safety net underneath me. I could freely be me and take risks. We worked hard together, and he taught me to make sure to take time to laugh—not just a little giggle but a laugh so hard that you can feel it in every part of your body.

He created the ultimate team environment. Every member of the team had strength and a specialty and was celebrated for bringing a unique voice to the table. We were all valued for our contribution, big or small, to the success of the team. Shelley radiated light! That is what amazing leaders do. They provide clarity and illuminate the path forward. Great leaders hold their torch high and radiate light and clarity—no shadows.

I was still sad, and I let myself be sad when learning about his passing. I wanted to feel what I needed to feel. I won't lie; it hurt. I just let myself be. I did the things that I knew to do to honor his memory and spirit. I dedicated that first yoga practice after learning about his passing to him and his lovely wife, Trudy. I helped host a celebration of his beautiful life with former colleagues and friends. That is what I knew to do to honor his spirit.

I kept going to my mat. That is where I work things out. There, I solve my problems, big and small. At times like that, I feel grateful for hot yoga. You can cry through an entire class, and no one really knows because you sweat so much. I just let myself be. I also worked really hard to make sure I dealt with what I felt. I talked with Mark, friends, and colleagues. Again, I went to my mat on my regular cadence purely for dedication to my practice.

A month or so after his passing, I had a terrific experience on my mat. My intention that evening was to show up, do my best, and do my work. I worked very hard that night and welcomed the gentle calm of Savasana. As I lay there on my back, I felt something lift off me. I can best describe the sensation as having a layer of darkness lift off me. It was dark and heavy. It rose off my body and lifted to the sky. As it lifted, it started to swirl. It swirled like a small, dark funnel cloud until, *poof*, it was gone.

As I rose up from Savasana to sit in a cross-legged pose, I felt better. I felt very much aware that this was a release. It marked a turning point in how I viewed Shelley's passing. I knew in my heart that he wouldn't want me to be sad and cry. He would want me to look back at and salute the great times we had. I can best honor his memory by practicing all the wonderful life lessons he taught me. I can also ensure that I do my best to be a Shelley to others around me and share the lessons he took the time to work through with me.

There are still times when I feel sad about his passing. I reframe looking back as a way to value the time I got to spend with him. I don't spend my energy on mourning his passing. Rest in peace, Shelley; rest in peace.

Chapter 22: *Leading with the Heart*

I have read two books in the last couple of years about leading with and from the heart. The first one is *Leading with the Heart* by the legendary coach Mike Krzyzewski (Krzyzewski 2000). The other one, *Lead from the Heart*, was written by my former colleague Mark Crowley (Crowley 2011). Leading from the heart is where my two worlds collide. Yoga is not about the asana, or the physical practice. Yoga is about how you think, or learning not to overthink. Yoga has helped me control my mind to direct my thoughts where I want them to go. As Beryl Bender Birch said, "This is truly mind control, control of our *own* minds" (Birch 1995, p. 196).

I'm no longer at the mercy of my monkey mind. Leading from the heart, to me, is all about sliding to the right side of my brain, connecting with people and their hearts, learning about them, and knowing what makes their heart sing. Magic happens when people emotionally tap into what they do and continue to surf and redefine their edges. One of my favorite books of all time is *Steve Jobs* by Walter Isaacson; the late Steve Jobs encouraged us to engage more than just the thinking, processing side of our brains (Isaacson 2011). So, the lesson here is to slide to the right. Get out of your head because, so often, thinking just hurts the team.

Connecting with people and helping them access what makes their hearts sing is amazing work. It gives our work meaning and answers why we do what we do. It's the connection that proves what you do is important. It drives you to get out of bed on those days that you could be easily swayed to stay in bed and pull the covers over your head.

When I started doing yoga, I felt broken. I was depressed. I found work cathartic and a great escape from the worries of my life. I had modest career success at the time but nothing to brag about. I remember on my first day as a financial advisor, a colleague of mine, Norm Levy, came to see me. Norm worked for Putnam Investments and still does. Norm came to see me with a beautiful bouquet of flowers and a kind word. He told me that the best advice he had for me was to be myself. If I had the courage to be who I really was, I would blow the doors off my business. It was great advice, but I had a problem.

I didn't believe that I was good enough. I let self-doubt creep in. In yoga, ironically, you have to go all the way into some poses to find stability. You can't go just halfway. You have to be all in. Two of the poses that I have to go all the way into to find my body's stability are the half-moon pose, or Ardha Chandrasana, and the revolved triangle pose, or Parivrtta Trikonasana. That's what Norm was telling me, but I didn't fully understand the message. I approached my new role in a tentative manner. Remember what Carla Harris says in her book *Strategize to Win*. I will repeat it because it's so powerful: "Fear has no place in your success equation; anytime that you operate from a position of fear, you will ALWAYS under penetrate that opportunity" (C. Harris 2014, 2339). Remember, you get back what you put out there. I wasn't giving my all, and in turn, I didn't see the results I was capable of.

One of my first and favorite lessons from yoga is that we are all born divine. I was born divine, and so were you. The informal definition of *divine* is "excellent or delightful." My first yoga teacher talked about being born divine in nearly every class. Mary Thomas went on to say that means I am good enough just the way I am. I don't have to do anything more to get there. I am everything I need to be, and I have everything I need just the way I am. I heard this class after class for the first couple of years. As I got better and stronger, I started to believe! Yoga helped me embrace my authentic self. If you are reading this book and haven't yet started on your journey, let me be the first to tell you that you were born divine as well. You are all you need to be, and you have everything you need. This marks an important step on your road to happiness. You don't need to do anything to be happy; you just need to be.

My initial transformation happened very fast. The first six months of my yoga practice went by in a blur. I emerged stronger in my body and my mind. I'm here to tell you that getting right in my body was in many ways easier than transforming my mind. But just like with physical workouts, when you keep working on getting right in your mind, that transformation happens as well.

I knew my mind was better when I started to become more truthful with myself. This could be as simple as acknowledging that I needed to rest out in poses or honoring the fact that I had not prepared well for a class. Maybe I hadn't eaten properly or drunk enough water. Being honest with yourself is the best way to begin honoring your authentic self.

As I started to emerge from the darkness, I became more honest with people around me. At one point, it concerned me that some would view my sharing my story and my experience as weakness—that I was broken and I needed help. I found just the opposite to be true. As I started to open up about these struggles or about the struggles I had with money early on in my life, people saw me as more real, and they could relate. I learned that it's all right to let people see the well-earned chinks in my armor. This is what Norm was saying: dare to be your beautiful, wonderful, fantastically flawed self. Put yourself out there, and you'll get rewarded. This is exactly what happened.

Where my confidence once waned, it came back in full force. I started to come into my true power. I was mindful of the fact that I've never put my full weight and force behind anything and failed. Not once has that ever happened in my personal or professional life. Now, that doesn't mean I haven't had failures. Of course, I have. I joke regularly I am good at my job because I have made every error one could possibly make on the journey.

The trick is I learn quickly from my errors and have the smarts to know when to course correct.

I read this crazy book by Tom Peters back in my early twenties called *Thriving on Chaos*. Just a side note: This was a dangerous book for someone so young to read. Man, I really felt ready to charge the mountain after reading his book. I remember that he says if you aren't making mistakes, then you aren't doing things right. In fact, he champions mistake making because it means you are clearly taking action. In the book, Peters says, "Numerous failures always (according to the laws of science) precede any success. Therefore, speeding up the success rate requires speeding up the failure rate" (Peters 1987, 476).

The yoga principle I think about here is what we talked about earlier: "Take your time, but take your time fast." The other key takeaway here is to learn quickly from your errors and not repeat them. You can't go on to learn your next lesson if you keep repeating your errors and don't learn the lessons you should learn on your path.

Chapter 23: *Living in the Present*

**Life moves pretty fast. If you don't stop
and look around once in a while, you could
miss it.**

—Ferris Bueller

Yoga is about being present. The best life happens in the present, in the moment. *Ferris Bueller's Day Off* is a fun movie about a character, Ferris, who celebrates taking time to live in the moment.

You can't do anything about the past except apply what you learn from your past to make your future better. You also miss what happens in the present when you spend too much time thinking and worrying about the future. Today is all that you are guaranteed. You'd be well advised to make the very most of the opportunity you have today. I observe far too many people planning for greatness tomorrow while dialing in their effort today.

I encourage you to act with urgency today, as if there won't be a tomorrow. This applies to whatever you choose to do, anything that matters to you.

When I was a little girl, we made memories. We had cameras, but you needed to be prepared to take pictures of events. You obviously needed a camera and film, and then you had to follow up to make sure the film got developed. Today is different, with the camera capabilities on our phones and devices. I do use my phone to document important or spontaneous moments, but I also continue what I learned when I was a little girl. I make a memory.

Making a memory teaches you to pause and take in the experience. Making a memory requires taking the time and energy to imprint every detail of the moment in your mind's eye. This includes the scene, what it sounds like, what it smells like, and what I feel in the moment. For me, making a memory is all about being present. When I go on vacation, I watch people wandering around taking pictures of everything or selfies in front of everything. I wonder if they are making the most of that moment. Are they really making a memory?

If you want to make memories, put down your device, and really connect. The best life happens in the present, in the moment. I understand the want to connect. We're more connected than ever. But I do question what you connect to. I'm not shirking technology. I do encourage you to pause and make sure that you make the most of real moments in your life. Make sure that your use of technology serves you. A good life happens in real time. If all the pictures and such imprint the memory for you, great! For me, it's a surface-level experience, glossing over taking the time to stay present to rush and share the experience on the social media site of the day.

Make sure you do not rob yourself of the opportunity to live in the moment and get the full experience the moment has to offer. Gary always says to "squeeze all the juice out of the orange" and enjoy every bite of it. This is what being mindful means to me. I loved the 2011 Toyota Venza commercial. In it, the parents are out living life and having adventures. The daughter sits in her apartment, admiring her connections on a social media site and watching cute cat videos. That was what really connecting was for her. She cites, "I have 687 friends—this is living." This is a great commercial and makes a good point.

At my core, I am a good listener and connector. Being a good listener is all about staying present. I find that as I mature with more responsibility at work and in my personal life, I have to make time to connect with others. There's something so powerful about looking someone directly in the eyes and really seeing and connecting with him or her. I get to do a lot of mentoring and coaching in my role as a leader. I love to look directly into the eyes of the person across from me and really connect—look right into his or her soul. I don't usually say this to people at work, but I tell them with my attention that the light in me honors the light I see in them. That's so powerful.

It's amazing how many times, in the quiet of those interactions, the other person becomes emotional. It represents a very real, honest connection. We need to foster more of this kind of connection. I get that different generations think and connect differently, but we must go out of our way to preserve quality in our human interactions. It's one of the best things about the human experience. So, put down your device, and really connect with someone. If you don't know how or where to start, go to a yoga class.

Chapter 24: *Making It Happen*

Yoga has taught me that I am stronger than I think. It has encouraged me to go places in my mind and body and try new things. News flash: This is true for me, and it's true for you as well. Here is the rub, though; you have to get off the couch and make it happen. The times when I feel the most alive occur when I make things happen. When I am on my yoga mat, giving 100 percent to my practice and myself, my heart beats, and I feel so healthy. I know my body loves the experience of being taken care of. My heart shows me that appreciation by pounding and pumping, showing me it's grateful for what I do for myself. It's my way of keeping my body bright and shiny, from the inside out.

Peter Avolio, my former yoga teacher, used to talk about your body being where you live. My body is where I live. It makes good sense that I need to do what I need to do to keep it clean, healthy, and in good working order. I work hard to ward off disease. I work hard to keep an ease in my body.

This doesn't just happen on my yoga mat. It happens on my

bike when I cycle. I find this on my mat and on my bike, but you might find it running, golfing, playing basketball, lifting weights, swimming, or whatever makes your heart sing. During a workout, on my mat or on my bike, I have those times when what I do challenges me. I hit that resistance point where I want to stop. As we said earlier, this is an edge. When you hang out near your edge, you can begin to push it out further. This is how we change, evolve, and stay relevant.

I deal with this on my bike in a couple of ways. Now, let me say I'm a serious yogi; I'm not as serious about my cycling. I do, however, believe that when I do something, I should take the time to do it well. I am a fair-weather cyclist. I start riding in April-ish (or when the rains let up in Seattle) and ride through September or maybe early October. I don't enjoy riding in extreme cold or rain.

I started riding around 2010 because a fellow leader asked me at an executive dinner if I would do the big ride for multiple sclerosis (MS), Bike MS (www.nationalmssociety.org). My ego said, "Of course," and not just the small ride. As I left the dinner that night, I kicked myself. I hadn't been on a bike since I was fifteen years old. I didn't even own a bike that would do the trick. I had to buy a bike and set about getting my legs ready to ride.

I fell in love with cycling. It's a great way to get me outdoors and enjoy the beautiful summer weather and clean air in Seattle. I upgraded to a road bike that rides so smoothly. I've been involved in the annual Bike MS nearly every year since. I was lucky that first year. I was lucky I didn't get hurt out there doing some serious riding with people who are very good at what they do.

I'm also the captain of our cycling team at work. In 2014, we decided to get involved with a ride called the WAVE (https:// thewavefoundation.org). The WAVE stands for "Women Against Violence Everywhere." It's a great cause. I joined the board to have a bigger impact. The WAVE mission is to educate, empower, and end domestic violence. It is built on the idea that strengthening women helps end domestic violence. The ride is for women only and is very well supported. Looking back, I should have started with that ride. It's a lot of fun and a safe ride every year. Women dress up in crazy outfits, and we just have fun and fundraise for a great cause. The ride has good attention to detail and great food at the end. The last rest stop features local firefighters. The firefighters cheer us on and give us Hot Tamale candies to keep us going.

In September 2015, our team rode the WAVE, the last official event of the season, and we determined which ride we would enjoy. The different rides are different distances, each with its own skill level. We opted for the Middle Sister ride. For several of the folks riding, it was the longest ride of their year with the highest degree of difficulty. All of us had ridden together throughout the training season. Spending all that time together, you get a feel for who can do what.

That was our second year doing the WAVE, and about six of us were riding. We showed up and pushed off. It was a beautiful day—a terrific day to enjoy the Northwest on a bike. About midway through, we lost one of our team members. She hadn't ridden much throughout the training season, and we lost her because her knee started hurting her. But we knew she was in terrific hands with the WAVE volunteers.

I closely watched two other teammates, Darcy Burns-Jelcz and Shawna Rexroat. They both are very nice people, and they questioned whether they should stop and support our team member dealing with knee pain. In any other situation, we all would have stopped together because we ride as a team. No worries with this ride, though, because it's so well supported. I adamantly told myself that Darcy and Shawna would not quit. Darcy and her husband, Mike, had started to train together, and finishing this ride was a big deal for Darcy. She'd gone out nearly every week and done her best getting her legs in shape. She'd gotten stronger every week, adding distance and speed every ride. Here is my point: Darcy had done the work in training and her conditioning.

The last leg of this ride is a little hillier than the rest of the ride. We literally rode right through my neighborhood. I knew it like the back of my hand. So, we pushed on. Darcy's mind questioned whether she should quit, but her body was fine. I stayed right on her. I told her I wouldn't let her quit. She was stronger than she realized, and I wanted her to focus on how good it would feel to finish. I encouraged her to think about how proud Mike, her husband, would be. This really got tough for Darcy. We slowed way down, and I stayed on her. She questioned out loud if she could finish. I kept telling her that she had enough strength to do this and the end was just around the next bend. Okay, I did lie a couple of times, but she needed that to not give up. She started to cry, but I made her keep on. Nothing worth doing is easy.

Darcy was on her edge, but I wanted her to see what she could do when she pushed beyond her edge. It frustrated her that I did lie a couple of times, but she understood what I was doing. I kept her eye on the prize—finishing—and how good it would feel to ride over that finish line. Darcy and Shawna did finish, and they both felt so proud of themselves. The point here is that they both had done the work and they deserved to finish because they could. Their bodies were plenty strong enough to finish; it was their minds that wanted to quit or give up. The best thing for both of them to do was not to think but to just do.

I use two more approaches when I feel that same way. Peter Avolio, my former yoga teacher and a serious cyclist, introduced me to the first approach during a yoga class. He yells out loud, "Shut up, legs!" The famous cyclist Jens Voigt is known for this approach. When he gets tired or on his edge, he yells, "Shut up, legs!" and powers on (Bicycling, 2014). When I feel tired or see someone on our cycling team struggling, I yell, "Shut up, legs!" at myself or at him or her. We laugh, but we know it reminds us that our minds are more restless than our bodies. Our bodies want to work hard, but we have to train our minds to stay strong.

I use something similar when I again get started on my bike after stopping for a rest. I learned this second technique with Gary Olson in the hot yoga room. It works like a charm. I use my imaging process to imagine that I haven't done anything and that I won't do anything. I ask myself what it would feel like to pretend I was just getting on my bike for the first time that day. It's a terrific technique. It's like hitting your own internal reset button. I use these two techniques to stay mentally tough on my bike. I remind myself on a regular basis when I ride how strong I am and what a lucky gal I am to get to go out and ride my bike.

Yoga planted one more important seed. It planted the seed while I was on my yoga mat but has served me well in my professional life. You have to believe that you can do whatever you set out to do. Belief is where everything starts. Gary Olson tells us every yoga class that you have to believe you can do it. Then you mindfully intend to do whatever you seek to do and put enough energy and effort into seeing that it gets done. This is really important and differentiates between wanting to do something and digging in and making it happen. Gary says, "Belief is nothing; desire is everything."

Chapter 25: *Avoid Overthinking*

I decided to take my own advice; thinking just hurts the team. A competing firm offered me a great job. The problem was I already have a great role at a terrific company. I thought about the opportunity and thought more about it. I reached out to a colleague and friend to ask for advice. I kept telling myself that I'd know what to do when the time was right. It was important to not just make something happen hastily. My friend reiterated that I would know what to do when the time came.

As soon as I got off the phone with him, I knew what to do; the time was right. The bottom line was the new firm needed me more than I needed them. That's why I had to think about things so much. If it had been right, it would've just felt right. I could easily have talked myself into the opportunity. The right thing to do was nothing. Sure, the offer had an upside, but the risk associated with the offer was the downside. Ultimately, the right thing for me to do was to stay put.

I am 100 percent sure I did the right thing by staying put. It's such a fine line between making things happen and having the discipline to let things unfold the way they are supposed to. The answer is found in staying mindful of the situation. Years ago, I would have pushed like a bull in a china shop and just jumped to take action.

Another example of applying this principle and avoiding overthinking comes up during the recruiting process. I do a lot of recruiting in my role. In fact, I would argue that recruiting is the single most important part of my role or of any leader's role. The bottom line is when you have the right people in the right seats, a leader's job gets easier, and the leader can work more effectively. When the leader fails to get the right people in the right seats, the whole work process becomes exceedingly more difficult and inefficient. Success boils down to putting the right people in the right seats with a good process.

Let me give you an example to illustrate my point. One time, flying back to my home in Seattle, I flew through a major airport. When I landed, I had time to wait before boarding the final flight. I knew it made good sense to grab a quick bite to eat before I boarded my flight back to Seattle. The airport was large with good signage and access to information about the amenities. I weighed my dining options and decided on Wendy's. As I made my way down the twenty gates to Wendy's, I happened upon a build-your-own-bowl eatery. It tickled me pink because this was a healthier choice than Wendy's. I was interested in this Mongolian grill–type setup's approach to managing its process, which was seemingly chaotic in the airport environment.

Almost from the get-go, I knew I was in trouble. Fortunately, I had time to wait and watch. One woman clearly was the leader. She barked out orders and reacted to what happened around her. Immediately, I saw that her team members didn't have a good understanding of their roles. They clearly had no process. A byproduct of this chaos was that the leader stepped in and tried to get everything done by herself. She had three other people around her. They looked lost, though. They kept getting assignments only to get reassignments very quickly. I watched this team struggle inefficiently for thirty minutes. All four members of the team struggled to find their flow because they clearly had no process. They really couldn't get things going in the right direction because they all made it up as they went along. Obviously, the leader really cared and tried to make things happen. Three other teammates who didn't care surrounded her.

One of the teammates may have cared, but she had given up. While I watched this scenario unfold, she was assigned and reassigned tasks at least four different times. She kept starting and stopping, no time to find a flow in any process. The other two individuals moved like turtles and clearly didn't care. It took thirty-two minutes from the time I paid to when I received my meal.

Two individuals actually walked away from this mess to take their breaks during the thirty-two minutes. This made an already chaotic situation worse. I watched the two of them move very slowly, not caring at all about their roles and the impact they had on the customers they served. I had four steps to my process, as a customer doing business with this company. I ordered, I paid, my meal was cooked to order, and ultimately I received the order. Although all four of the workers touched my process, the leader came through and made every step actually happen, while the others wandered around, not really doing anything and certainly not caring.

This experience tested my patience. It frustrated me and made me connect to why people take to social media sites to share their frustration. I didn't want to contribute to that nonsense. Instead, I opted to use this as an example to illustrate my point. This leader clearly cared about what she did. She didn't efficiently get the work done through and with the other three people. They clearly didn't care, which I will address in a moment, and they lacked any clear process. People like process. It helps get things done. When you lack process, everything gets managed as an exception. It's an inefficient way to operate.

Another important issue here is caring. Caring is one of those traits that you either have or you don't have. I, as a leader, can't teach you or anyone to care. This is why the recruiting process, or recruiting cycle, has so much importance. It is a leader's opportunity to see what he or she is really getting—the good, the bad, and the ugly. Recruiting is a lot like dating used to be for me. I'd meet men and see how they could be. I had to kiss a lot of frogs before I found my prince. Along the way, I learned that men are the way men are. When you've made your partner selection, you'll get what you get! You're fooling yourself if you think this man you chose will change. People are the same way. They are how they are.

When I was newer to leadership, I would ask myself—no, better yet, I would talk myself into—why someone could do the job based on their experience and credentials. This involved a thinking process, yet another example of thinking hurting the team. The better question I have learned to asked myself is this: Will this person do the job? I still use the same standard questions for each person. I have learned to tune in to how I feel about a person and to trust my instincts. My instincts tell me how I feel about my interactions with this person. This is important because how I feel about this person will largely reflect the experiences my clients and colleagues eventually will have with this individual.

Now, I'm thoughtful of how I feel, and trust my instincts when I am with an individual I am recruiting. I'm also mindful that if people approach the recruiting process properly, I'm seeing them on their best behavior. It won't go uphill from the interview. Thinking too much about this process can hurt you and your team. It is important to learn as much as you can in the recruiting cycle so you can select wisely and add someone who will contribute positively and care about his or her success and ultimately your team's success. Choose wisely; your career and reputation largely rest on your ability to do so.

Chapter 26: *Dream Big*

Yoga is all about being present. The best life happens in the moment; in fact, all life happens in the present moment. Yoga is all about getting and being right with you. Yoga has been a fabulous journey into me—who I am and what I am capable of. Yoga has helped me delve into myself and pull out the best parts. It all starts here. This is how you engage your authentic self and start to bring that self to work. I have to be at my very best to ask people to follow me or have the capacity to take care of the folks who do. I have honed the following steps on my yoga mat that I bring into the boardroom to drive success. It's a simple four-step process.

1. **Dream big dreams.** Remember, you're capable of doing more than you're doing—capable of greatness. Protect your flame, and learn how to direct your spark the right way. Be very careful about what you think about because what you think about comes true. This is true for

the good things you think about and the bad things you worry about.

2. **Turn your dreams into goals.** Once you see your dreams as goals, begin to plan the steps to achieve those goals. Then monitor your progress and adjust your plans accordingly.

3. **Believe.** I am a huge proponent of positive self-talk. You have to believe you can do whatever you set out to do. Then you have to put in all the energy and effort it takes to make it happen. This is true for whatever you choose to do in life. Again, be careful and mindful of what you tell yourself. Your self-talk is like a recorder; during tough times, you will hear back exactly what you have told yourself. During those stressful times, you don't need to hear, "I'm not good enough" or "I suck." My go-to mantra for many years is "I've got this!" During tough times, I hear myself tell me exactly that.

4. **Understand that desire is where it all happens.** This is the big one and the difference maker. The other three steps are easy; anyone can do all three. Desire means going out and doing the heavy lifting to make sure that you do the hard work to make it happen. This is all about your grit, what you are made of. This is what you are willing to do when no one is watching. This is where you find your edge and use your fire to reshape and redefine what your edge looks like.

Dream big dreams, and turn your dreams into goals. Believe in yourself, and understand that it all happens by having the desire to make it happen. Be willing to put in the hard work and effort needed to make what you want to happen a reality. That is the recipe for a life well lived. It all starts with you and what you are willing to do to get things done.

Your life is all about the decisions and choices you make, good and bad. That's my truth, and it's true for you as well. I've also learned that the choices I make in life are not nearly as important as what I make of my choices. One of my favorite expressions is "It is what it is." I love the late coach Pat Summitt's take on this phrase. Here's what she used to tell her basketball team: "It is what it is. But, it will be what you make it."

Yoga helps me make better, well-thought-out choices in my life. When I know better, I do better. This tool has served me exceedingly well at work. It will continue to serve me well throughout the rest of my career. I have a good ten years left in me in the corporate environment. Then I will downshift at work and spend more time in an Ashram somewhere, standing on my head and sharing all the goodness this lifestyle has to offer by teaching.

Yoga means union. My time on my mat gets me close to source, close to my flame and fire. It's the same flame that burns in you. It's your ignition source or spark that, when directed properly, can fuel something more powerful, should you flip your switch. When you manage it properly, you can direct your flame into fire. It all starts by having enough bravery to reach out and touch your flame. It's important to become the protector of your flame. Without fierce protection, it's easy to extinguish your flame. It is hard to reignite your flame once it has gotten snuffed out. You also run the risk of your flame getting put out forever. Your flame is just the start of what you are capable of. It represents your creative spirit, and to loosely quote Steve Jobs, it's your ability to make a dent in the universe.

The light in me honors the bright light in you. Shine on, and shine brightly. Namaste.

Resource Guide

I remember how intimidated I felt to go into a yoga room and not know anything. The great news is that you can use your Google power and research anything you want in preparation of taking a yoga class. My advice is that you find someone like me and just ask him or her where he or she practices and why. People who love where they practice will usually tell you what classes and teachers you should try. I love hot yoga, but I also understand that hot yoga isn't for everyone.

I am always willing to take anyone with me to a yoga practice. It's always great to share the experience with someone who's new to the process. Remember, we all had our first class once. I recommend that you take three classes before you make up your mind on how you feel about yoga. Sometimes, the first experience can overwhelm you, but every experience after that gets better.

If you live in Seattle or Bellevue, I encourage you to check out The Ashram (http://theashramyoga.com). You will have a better experience if you are hydrated. Make sure you bring a mat, a towel, and water to class with you. You might consider getting a towel called a Yogitoe (www.manduka.com/yoga-towels/yogitoes-towels.html). Yogitoe towels are great because they reduce the risk of falling from slipping. The knob-like things on them go face down on your mat. I always put a little water on the towel where my hands and feet go in downward-facing dog. The moisture sets the towel so that you won't slip. You can also consult the website for your yoga studio to see if they rent mats and towels.

I would also suggest that you arrive early to your first class. Let the instructor know that you are new to the process. You'll also want to let the instructor know how your body feels. The great thing about yoga is it's accessible to everyone. If you let the instructor know what is going on in your body, he or she can make recommendations that may work better for your body.

One of the best things about going through yoga teacher training was I got to revisit anatomy. I know I must have taken an anatomy class in school, but I needed a refresher course. The amazing Tina Templeman here in Seattle teaches anatomy for yoga in yoga studios across the country. I have enjoyed her class so much more since I've known more about how my body works. I also now work with weights as part of my overall fitness plan. It is critical to know where each muscle is and how to activate it.

Tina recommended a book called *The Key Muscles of Yoga* by Ray Long. It is easy to read and has lots of pictures. I enjoyed this book so much that I read the second book in the series, *The*

Key Poses of Yoga, also by Ray Long. If you need a more in-depth look at yoga anatomy, check out *Yoga Anatomy* by Leslie Kaminoff and Amy Matthews.

During yoga teacher training, I found a terrific book called *The Language of Yoga* by Nicolai Bachman. The book includes definitions and a pronunciation guide for the terms and asanas. The book starts out with an explanation of what Sanskrit is and why it's important. Bachman says, "This sacred language originated from oral traditions developed to communicate the spiritual insights of ancient sages" (Bachman 2005, 1). Sanskrit is the language of yoga. It is important information for anyone serious about studying yoga.

My sister-in-law Cheryl Schwarzwalter gave me a terrific gift that folks new to yoga would find helpful. It is a book called *2,100 Asanas* by Daniel Lacerda. It's a picture book of all the asanas or poses. It was a thoughtful gift that I appreciate.

The best way to learn more about yoga is to go out, try different yoga styles, and find the one that fits you. You have to have experience to get experience. Your mind and body will thank you.

The following are the resources mentioned in this section.

- Nicolai Bachman, *The Language of Yoga: Complete A to Y Guide to Āsana Names, Sanskrit Terms, and Chants* (Boulder, CO: Sounds True, 2005).
- Leslie Kaminoff and Amy Matthews, *Yoga Anatomy*, 2nd ed. (Champaign, IL: Human Kinetics, 2012).

- Daniel Lacerda, *2,100 Asanas: The Complete Yoga Poses* (New York: Black Dog & Leventhal, 2015).
- Ray Long, *The Key Muscles of Yoga: Your Guide to Functional Anatomy in Yoga* (Baldwinsville, NY: Bandha Yoga, 2005).
- Ray Long, *The Key Poses of Yoga: Your Guide to Functional Anatomy in Yoga* (Baldwinsville, NY: Bandha Yoga, 2008).

References

Bachman, Nicolai. *The Language of Yoga: Complete A to Y Guide to Āsana Names, Sanskrit Terms, and Chants.* Boulder, CO: Sounds True, 2005.

Bicycling. "The Origin of 'Shut Up, Legs!'" May 17, 2014. www.bicycling.com/video/origin-shut-legs.

Birch, Beryl Bender. *Power Yoga: The Total Strength and Flexibility Workout.* New York: Fireside, 1995.

Bossidy, Larry, and Charan, Ram. *Execution: The Discipline of Getting Things Done.* New York: Crown Business, 2002.

Chetner, Marina. "How to Tame Your Monkey Mind." *MindBodyGreen.* July 19, 2012. www.mindbodygreen.com/0-5507/How-to-Tame-Your-Monkey-Mind.html.

Crowley, Mark C. *Leading from the Heart: Transformational Leadership for the 21st Century.* Bloomington, IN: Balboa Press, 2011.

Duckworth, Angela. *Grit: The Power of Passion and Perseverance.* New York: Scribner, 2016.

Duhigg, Charles. *Smarter Faster Better: The Transformative Power of Real Productivity.* New York: Random House, 2016.

Eat Taste Heal. "Ayurveda 101: The Three Doshas—The Keys to Your Individual Nature." Accessed March 20, 2017. www.eattasteheal.com/ayurveda101/eth_bodytypes.htm.

Estés, Clarissa Pinkola. *Women Who Run with the Wolves: Myths and Stories of the Wild Woman Archetype.* New York: Ballantine Books, 1992.

Greenspan, Alan. *The Age of Turbulence: Adventures in a New World.* New York: Penguin, 2007.

Harris, Carla. *Strategize to Win: The New Way to Start Out, Step Up, or Start Over in Your Career.* New York: Hudson Street Press, 2014.

Harris, Dan. *10% Happier: How I Tamed the Voice in My Head, Reduced Stress without Losing My Edge, and Found Self-Help That Actually Works.* New York: HarperCollins, 2014.

Isaacson, Walter. *Steve Jobs.* New York: Simon & Schuster, 2011.

Iyengar, B.K.S. *Light on Yoga.* New York: Schocken, 1979

Krzyzewski, Mike. *Leading with the Heart: Coach K's Successful Strategies for Basketball, Business, and Life.* New York: Warner Business Books, 2000.

McKeown, Greg. *Essentialism: The Disciplined Pursuit of Less.* New York: Crown Business, 2014.

Murray, Nick. *The Game of Numbers: Professional Prospecting for Financial Advisors.* Author, 2010.

Myss, Caroline. *Sacred Contracts: Awakening Your Divine Potential.* Harmony Books, 2011.

Peters, Tom. *Thriving on Chaos: Handbook for a Management Revolution.* New York: Knopf, 1987.

Reuters. "Market Yogis: Financial Planners Take Up Yoga." March 8, 2016. www.reuters.com/article/ us-investing-advisers-yoga-idUSKCNOWA1R1 4?utm_source-applenews.

Sadhguru. "Why Disease? What Is It? Where Does It Come From?" January 8, 2008. https://ishayoga.word-press.com/2008/01/08/why-disease-what-is-it-wher e-does-it-come-from.

Williams, Mabel, and Dalphin, Marcia, eds. *The Young Folks' Shelf of Books.* New York: P. F. Collier & Son, 1960.

Yoga.org.nz. "Definition of Yoga." Accessed March 20, 2017. http://yoga.org.nz/what-is-yoga/yoga_definition.htm.

About the Author

Salisa R. Roberts, CFP®, is a senior leader at one of the nation's largest regional, bank-based financial services companies. Throughout her twenty-eight-year career in financial services, she has proven that success and happiness in a traditional business environment require a balance of both hard and soft skills.

Salisa has practiced yoga for sixteen years. She has worked to bring the principles she has learned in the yoga room into the boardroom.

When Salisa is not working or doing yoga, she enjoys reading, cycling, cooking and writing. Salisa and her husband, Mark, live in Bellevue, Washington, with their two cats, Riley and Shy.

Printed in the United States
By Bookmasters